WRITING YOUNG ADULT NOVELS

Hadley Irwin and
Jeannette Eyerly

Writer's
Digest
Books

Cincinnati, Ohio

Writing Young Adult Novels. Copyright © 1988 by Hadley Irwin and Jeannette Eyerly. Printed and bound in the United States of America. All rights reserved. No part of this book may be reproduced in any form or by any electronic or mechanical means including information storage and retrieval systems without permission in writing from the publisher, except by a reviewer, who may quote brief passages in a review. Published by Writer's Digest Books, an imprint of F&W Publications, Inc., 1507 Dana Ave., Cincinnati, Ohio 45207. First edition.

---

92 91 90 89 88   5 4 3 2 1

Library of Congress Cataloging-in-Publication Data

Irwin, Hadley.
  Writing young adult novels/Hadley Irwin and Jeannette Eyerly. p.   cm.
  Bibliography: p.
  Includes index.
  ISBN 0-89879-313-0
  1. Young adult fiction—Authorship. I. Eyerly, Jeannette. II. Title.
PN3377.I77 1988   87-29790
808.06'8—dc19   CIP

Design by Alice Mauro

CONTENTS

♦

Foreword

one
KNOW THE TERRITORY · 3

It helps to know the traditions of Young Adult fiction; the past can offer suggestions for innovation. Here's a quick historical perspective.

two
CHOOSE YOUR GENRE · 11

Romance, history, science fiction, mystery, and more—each direction provides a special way of telling *your* story. Each genre has its own conventions, and the alternatives are exciting.

three
WHO'S YOUR READER AND WHO ARE YOU? · 23

The writer-reader connection is the avenue to success. Take time to understand the value of your own life experience; then analyze your audience.

four
BEFORE YOU TOUCH THE KEYS · 33

Writing *is* a trip, but to get and give the most, you need to plan your journey—to make a mental map. Planning time and thinking time will make story telling more effective.

five
IN THE BEGINNING · 49

You'll create a world for your readers, but unless the first sentence is an invitation to enter, they won't turn the page. Dialogue, action, and description are just the beginning of beginnings.

six
WHAT A CHARACTER! · 67

Your story will be populated with people, but cardboard characters don't breathe. Discover techniques of creating three dimensions on the printed page; your reader must identify with your characters.

seven
HOW LONG IS HIS HAIR? HOW SHORT IS HER SKIRT? · 81

From historical fiction to contemporary problem novel, social customs, language, hair lengths, and hem lengths must be accurate. Stay in synch with the styles of your time frame.

eight
HE SAID, SHE SAID · 91

Writing honest dialogue can be tricky, but it becomes easier if you know the basic rules. Develop an ear for the way people speak, get to know your characters, then listen to what *they* have to say.

nine
MIDDLES—USING PRIME TIME · 103

Half your readers' fun is finding out *how* events evolve; the middle of a book is its heart. Keep your reader excited by plot, subplot and pace.

ten
HOW TO GET FROM THE HOUSE TO THE BARN · 123

The shortest transition in time or setting can take the longest time to write. Here are some shortcuts that can take you quickly from here to there, from place to place or from time to time.

eleven
ALL'S WELL THAT ENDS WELL · 133

Wrap up the loose ends, create a satisfying final scene, leave your reader content but wishing that the story continue. You can make your characters live on in the minds of your audience; after all, the writer has the last word.

twelve
TENSE, TONE, VOICE, AND MOOD · 143

Beyond plot, character, and theme, language exerts its own power over the reader. Words themselves evoke emotion, create atmosphere, set up suspense. Your dictionary can be your best friend.

thirteen
REVISING AND REWRITING · 153

Fine tuning makes a motor run smoothly and your readers will appreciate your ability with mechanics. Revision and rewriting can be one of the pleasures of the creative process—it's the chance to move from *what* you want to say to *how* you want to say it.

fourteen
HIDDEN MESSAGES/HIDDEN DANGERS · 165

Even with the best of intentions, you may convey negative stereotypes, thoughtless biases, and attitudes you didn't intend. Once you know what to look for, you can avoid some rough spots.

fifteen
YOU'RE ON YOUR WAY · 173

Parting with a manuscript can be as difficult as beginning one. The best cure for post-writing depression is the United States Postal Service. Mail that manuscript!

RULES AND REMINDERS · 181

Here's a checklist of the basics; they soon become part of the writer's subconscious.

APPENDIX · 183

SUGGESTED READING · 187

INDEX · 190

AUTHORS' NOTE

Although the material in this book, as the title indicates, pertains to the art of novel writing, particularly the novel slanted toward the young adult reader, much of it is applicable to short stories as well. In short stories as in novels, the characters must be believable, dialogue must ring true, and the plot, though not as complex, must be carefully crafted. The mechanics of transition, scene, and summary, point of view and the necessity of revision are, likewise, as important to the creation of a successful short story as they are to the novel.

Each type of fiction tells a story; each has a beginning, a middle, and an end. How long that story will be depends on the strength and complexity of the idea that prompted it. As most ideas "grow" if carefully nurtured, we suggest you aim for the longer length. The short story market, in general, is limited; the market for the young adult short story is more limited still.

FOREWORD

◆

The three of us—Annabelle Irwin and Lee Hadley, who write together as Hadley Irwin, and Jeannette Eyerly—first met at a state library meeting where we had been invited to appear and autograph our books. Afterward, there was only time for us to say how much we admired each other's work and agree to meet again. Soon after, we did that, and as a result became good friends.

No one now remembers who said it first, but there the question was, hanging in the air: "If the three of us know so much, why don't we write a book?"

Within seconds we had a title and a subtitle—which we later regretfully discarded in favor of one less clever and more practical—and within fifteen minutes we had an outline of fifteen chapters.

We laid down no ground rules. As soon as a chapter was written, we had copies made and mailed them to each other for criticism. With two novels in progress, we could set no time table for getting together again. When we could, we would.

Meanwhile chapters and pieces of chapters, accompanied by letters headed "Dear Author," began circulating. As the pile of manuscript began to grow, so did our satisfaction. Although we occasionally got together for a rally and a good visit, we decided to do no major tinkering until we reached the end. That, we said, would be the day—and it was, with "the day" managing to turn into months as we went through the laborious process of revision and rewriting.

Some chapters were too short and needed additional material. Some needed surgery, a good deal of which was accomplished with scissors and cellular tape. Chunks were lopped off here and transferred there. Several chapters were added while others disappeared entirely—only to appear in new guise elsewhere. The list of Most-Asked Questions grew as did the list of Rules and Reminders.

When at last it was finished, we discovered a surprising thing. Although our original intention was to provide a guide for writing the Young Adult Novel, we found we had also written a book that would help any aspiring novelist. We knew that college professors—as two of us were and are—would find it useful, not only in teaching Creative Writing classes but in guiding students through the maze of courses in Young Adult Literature. English and Language Arts teachers at the senior and junior high levels had already used certain chapters in their writing classes.

In other words, the "whole" turned out to be greater than the "sum of its parts." And so we give it to you for any purpose you choose. We suggest you not waste time trying to figure out which one of us has written what. Our book titles will give you no clue. Frequently we write about the other's books. The best thing to do is get busy and *write*.

Hadley Irwin

Jeannette Eyerly

one

KNOW THE TERRITORY

———◆———

The world of Young Adult literature is relatively new, and though it's full of unexplored areas that offer fascinating possibilities for you as a writer, it's also helpful to have a chart of what has come before. Like a traveler, you must know where you've been before you can clearly know where you are going.

Let's start with a definition of the goal. Young Adult fiction is written BY a serious author, FOR a young adult reader, ABOUT the problems, emotions, and events that concern adolescents. YA writing bridges the gap between the child and the adult. That bridge was built in the 1930s.

In earlier years, teens were reading books written *about* adolescents, *by* adults, *for* adults: Alcott's *Little Women*, Twain's *Huckleberry Finn*, Stevenson's *Treasure Island*. A few alternatives existed in series books about Nancy Drew, the Hardy Boys, or Tom Swift, all of whom were stereotyped characters involved in predictable plots with lots of action. Teachers feared that readers of this "subliterature" would never progress past the excitement of the formula story to appreciate the classics. Liberal critics argued that readers would tire of series books and move on to other literature.

Time was right in the early 1930s for adolescent fiction to emerge as a distinct genre. Whether Boylston's *Sue Barton, Stu-*

dent Nurse or Rose Wilder Lane's *Let the Hurricane Roar* was the first true adolescent novel matters little, but the success of such books was real. It may seem a long stretch from *Sue Barton* to Judy Blume's *Deenie,* but from the middle of the thirties on, writers flooded the market with books and stories for young adults.

Publishers soon had to set off special sections in their catalogs labeled "Juvenile Literature," and libraries, both public and school, followed suit by designating shelves and special rooms for the young adult reader. Perhaps the term "Juvenile Literature" was not the best term for the phenomenon. One adult remarked recently that when she was eleven her mother suggested she go into the juvenile section of the local library instead of continuing to select her books from the children's section. After being pressed for a reason for not doing so, she told her mother, "I thought that room was for delinquents."

English teachers, of course, welcomed the new juvenile classification. It was the missing rung in the ladder of reading, aiding the young reader to step from picture books of childhood to the more sophisticated offerings for adults. And when inexpensive, readily available paperbacks appeared with works specifically written for teenagers, teachers could place emphasis on individual reading tastes and get students "hooked on books."

By the fifties, adolescent literature occupied a place of its own in schools, libraries, and publishing houses, but there were some rather strict rules about writing such novels: no dirty words, no explicit sexual situations, no challenges to the values set up by the establishment. The novels of the fifties usually had a definite theme: growing up, discovering oneself, playing fair, with the story usually set a year or two ahead of the intended reader's age. Characters were often flat, definitely middle-class, and usually limited to two or three. Plots were simple, had few flashbacks, and often concerned school proms, football games, cheerleading tryouts, and such. The writing was rich with narrative and dialogue, with things really getting off to a running start in the first chapter. Most of the stories were predictable, so that the young reader never had to wonder *how* the plot would turn out, but only *when* the happy ending would be reached.

The sixties changed all this. Teachers, librarians, publishers, and the young readers demanded better books with real characters and lifelike problems. The real world did not tie up everything into neat little happy endings. All girls did not want to be cheerleaders. All boys did not strive to win the big game for the "Gipper." There were real stories to be found in the ghettos of Chicago, among the migrant workers of California. Families were often broken by divorce; parents were alcoholics. Realism moved into young adult literature in the sixties and seventies. The titles speak to this: *Drop Out, Dinky Hocker Shoots Smack, Mom, the Wolf Man and Me, My Dad Lives in a Downtown Hotel, My Darling, My Hamburger, Pardon Me You're Stepping on my Eyeballs.* Sex. Drugs. Abortion. War. Premarital sex. Child abuse. No phony conclusions. Tell it like it is. In other words, writers were being forced to treat their young readers with respect and not sugarcoat the realities of the world.

Realism forced publishers and allowed writers of young adult novels to look beyond middle-class, white America. Lorenz Graham, one of the first writers to portray realistic black characters facing the problems of discrimination in *South Town* (1958), *North Town* (1965), and *Whose Town?* (1969), paved the way for writers to pursue their various ethnic interests.

Realism and its stepchild, the "problem novel," have persisted through the 1970s and well into the 1980s, but another type of adolescent novel has emerged—the teen romance, which is in many ways reminiscent of the 1950 romances of Betty Cavanna's *Going on Sixteen* and Anne Emery's *Going Steady.* Again publishers are jumping on the new trend with a flood of serial publications bred from the popular success of the adult Harlequin romance and the appeal of TV's soap operas. These new young adult romances sport such alluring series titles as *Sunfire, Sweet Dreams, Sweet Valley High,* and *Turning Points.* The pattern, formulaic, features continuing characters, a more superficial treatment of problems than are faced in the realistic problem novels, and cliff hangers similar to the Nancy Drew series. The romances are usually written on a fifth or sixth grade reading level for girls from ten to fifteen, and can be read in about two hours. These romances echo the same taboos of the 1950s: no explicit sex, no locker-room words, "squeaky clean" characters, and always a happy ending.

Among teenage girls, these books are tremendously popular, perhaps because they offer a short escape from the real world. A quick look at the shelves of any book store will show you that they are in demand by a very large and faithful audience.

CRITICISM

What will keep you honest, as a potential author of YA literature, are a number of publications to be found today that devote space to the criticism and evaluation of new books. Along with a background of YA literature, a writer should be a constant reader of such publications as *Publishers Weekly, New York Times Book Review, The Alan Review* (a publication of the National Council of Teachers of English), *Booklist* (American Library Association), *Horn Book, Kirkus Reviews, Media and Methods, School Library Journal, Voice of Youth Advocates* (VOYA), and *Interracial Books for Children Bulletin.*

Perhaps the one event that has assured young adult novels a place of their own is the inclusion of courses in adolescent literature in the university curricula for future teachers and librarians. As a result, numerous textbooks on adolescent literature have appeared that can provide a rich source of background material for a writer. We can recommend *Literature for Today's Young Adults* (Donelson and Nilsen; Scott, Foresman), *Reaching Adolescents: The Young Adult Book and the School* (Althea Reed; Holt, Rinehart and Winston), *Children's Literature: An Issues Approach* (Rudman; Longman), *A Guide to Literature For Young Adults* (Cline and McBride: Scott Foresman).

AWARDS

The "Oscar" for YA literature is the prestigious John Newbery Medal, presented annually to a book judged to be the most outstanding work for that year. A committee selected by the American Library Association, Children's Service Division, read quantities of new works nominated by librarians across the country. Receiving the Newbery or having a book named as a Newbery

Honor Book is tantamount to not only immediate, but lasting, success. There are a variety of other awards that are waiting for writers. Various states have their own Children's Choice List for which school librarians compile titles for the year and from which young readers make a selection of their favorites. Other awards include the ALA Best Book List, Golden Kite Award (Society of Writers of Children's Books), Jane Addams Peace Association Award for Children's Literature, the Award for Children's Literature from the Society of Midwest Authors. To see how far young adult literature has come, you can obtain a paperback publication that lists all such awards: *Awards and Prizes: Children's Book Council,* 175 Fifth Avenue, New York City, NY 10010.

CAN YOU WRITE FOR YOUNG ADULTS?

You may feel that you are light years beyond your own adolescence and completely out of touch with today's teenagers. Association with this age group can be helpful. Perhaps having taught in junior high and high school is an advantage, as is having reared children, but if this were an absolute, all YA novels would be written by parents and teachers. This is not the case. As one successful writer said, "It's enough to have survived your own adolescence."

You must understand that young readers are in many ways just as knowledgeable as adults. They love, hate, hope, fear, envy, admire. The only difference is that the teenager has not lived very long. You, as a would-be author, must not write down to this audience. They are just as intelligent as grown-ups; all they lack is experience.

Margaret Early in 1960 outlined three stages of growth in the development of a reader. At first, a child reads for the pure, unconscious joy of reading. Along about junior high, the child begins to identify personally with the characters and becomes a vicarious participant in the story. A child of this age is basically egocentric, concerned with self and establishing an identity. The last stage, the most difficult to attain, is the appreciation of the aesthetic value in the story: deeper meanings, techniques of presentation, theme, and its relationship to humankind.

The YA novel is aimed at the reader in Early's second stage: the stage of finding out "Who am I?" As in climbing a ladder, the child must not be pressured to skip this second rung and attempt to appreciate a work beyond comprehension. Skipping the "Who am I?" stage can turn a would-be reader into a nonreader. Thus, the YA novel must focus on concerns appropriate to young readers.

Don't worry about controlling your vocabulary. The character about whom you are writing will control it. Young adults read what interests them; if they come upon an unfamiliar word, they will usually deduce the meaning from the context and add a new word to their vocabulary in the process. Write to the best of your ability. Write for the teenager in all of us—from eight to eighty.

Writers once believed that girls would read books about boys, but boys would not read books about girls. With the discovery that individual differences were more influential than sex differences in the choosing of a book, writers reassessed this theory. A book is either a "good read" for a teenager or it's, as they say, "BORING!" If characters are fully developed and believable, your young readers won't mind whether the book is about a boy or a girl.

No author should look down on the young adult novel as a mere exercise to be dashed off or as an entry level activity before attempting an adult novel. Writing for young adults demands the same careful crafting, the same precise language skills, the same artistic care as that demanded by any piece of literature. Many writers chafe at the label of juvenile or adolescent literature. Writers of young adult books write for people—people who happen to be young and people who have been young.

If there is a difference between a young adult novel and an adult novel it is in length. YA books usually range from 35,000 words on up; the adult novel begins at about 60,000 words. Keeping a novel to the length that will appeal to a young reader is a difficult challenge acknowledged by the wit who wrote to a friend, "If I had more time, I would have written a shorter letter."

As a prospective writer for young adults, you must be completely *honest* with your reader. You must have something to say and believe in what you are saying without being judgmental or attempting to moralize. Young readers can spot fakey plots, unrealistic solutions, and contrived situations at a glance, and they can be more severe critics than the most highly touted reviewer. On the other hand, they can be more vocal in their praise. When you write as honestly as you can about something you feel strongly about, your "message" will come through loud and clear.

You must also have the highest *respect* for the young reader. It is a grave error to assume that you must write down to this audience, either in subject matter, vocabulary, style, or situation. Write the story you, yourself, want to read, the story you wanted to read when you were in your teens. One writer remarked, "At fourteen, I thought I knew all I needed to know about the world. Strangely enough, I was right in most cases." Teenage readers want books with vivid, real worlds, full of information, fun and excitement, exactly what any adult reader demands from a book.

Writers for young adults should have *empathy* with teenagers, an understanding of this age which is fraught with the peculiar problems of growing up, and a good memory of their own adolescence. Even though today's teenage problems concern drugs and abortion, instead of hot rods and prom queens, the degree of concern is no less. In the process of creating a character for a young adult novel, you will come to a new understanding of teenagers and an appreciation of their fads and fancies and escapades. With understanding comes tolerance and love.

A fresh, original, and imaginative *sense of humor* is a must. Teenagers read for fun, for surprise, for suspense: the basis of humor. Comedy can be serious. Tragedy can be ironic, if not funny. Your book doesn't have to be an overall comedy, but it must be spiced with lines that at least can evoke a chuckle now and then.

GET SET, GO

How exciting to be a part of a literary mode that has been in existence for a mere half century. Enrich your own background by going back and reading some of those novels from the thirties, forties, and fifties. See for yourself the refinement and development of this art form. Reread your favorite book from your own teenage years. Can you remember your "rotten year"? Can you reexperience the feelings and emotions and events that you knew you could never survive? So now, you want to write for that ambivalent age! If you survived adolescence, you can write for this audience, but first you must know the territory.

With all the territory of the Young Adult Novel now laid out, you may feel that there is no new ground to be explored. Not true. Books are being written today that were undreamed of yesterday, and books on subjects undreamed of today will be written tomorrow. Yesterday's territory is still there, waiting for those with an observant eye, a fresh viewpoint, and a lively imagination. Tomorrow's territory is still to be explored.

· two ·

CHOOSE YOUR GENRE

---◆---

Just as life is a matter of choosing among alternatives, so is writing. In either case, the choice is dictated by a number of things: one's background, personal preference, goals, and sometimes contemporary pressures. The result of one's choice, may, in the case of writing, be a long and successful career.

Young adult literature, though somewhat ambiguous in nature, does exist and has existed for quite a few years and will go on evolving and changing as long as there are writers and readers and publishers. However, under the general category of YA, the choices of genres are many. As in any attempt to classify types of writing, the genres are not necessarily mutually exclusive, but certain kinds of books promise particular elements to readers and usually adhere, however loosely, to general patterns.

READER'S CHOICE

Today what teenagers choose to read is dictated less by parents, librarians, and teachers than by what peers are reading, enjoying, and talking about. Kids take advice from one another when it comes to choosing a book. You as an author must know *what* they are reading. Talk to librarians. They can tell you what kinds of books move most rapidly from their shelves. Cull the latest market lists from publishers. You'll find what is expected to do well. Not that you have to follow the latest trend, for if a book is good, someone will eventually publish it.

Think of your own reading history. Wasn't there a time in which, at least for a while, you were reading nothing but horse stories, dog stories, historical romances or series books? The same is true for today's readers. The secret is to find the kind of book you are comfortable with and excited about.

Those are basically the same criteria your audience will use in selecting the books they read.

WRITER'S CHOICE

What kind of novel should you write? You have a wide choice: problem/character, mystery, Gothic, fantasy, science fiction, myth, legend, adventure, sport, historical, career, animal, romance, and endless combinations and varieties of all of these.

The most important thing to remember, when you are thinking about the story that you will write, is that all stories, no matter what the genre, no matter what the plot, no matter what the events, are based on people acting. Perhaps the basis of all narrative is the combination of noun and verb. All the rest is embellishment. Noun and verb are craft; the rest is art or drivel.

A writer must develop double vision. You must write about what you care for, what you know about or can research, about human situations or behavior that interests you. At the same time, if you want to be published, you must think about your potential market. Consider some of the alternatives, then see how and where your particular story idea seems to find a home.

Problem/Character Novel

An editor told a first-time writer who had sent him a manuscript, "I like your work, but we're more interested in character novels than problem novels." She was baffled, but with rethinking and rewriting, her book was published by that same editor.

It's a matter of emphasis. A novel may illustrate a problem without sufficient characterization in which case the writer has probably chosen a theme because it's been highly publicized: on the other hand, it would be possible, though improbable, to create a book with a character who does not have a problem, or if so, doesn't recognize the fact. The last story of that sort that we can remember is that of Pollyanna, who resolved everything with her "happy" game.

At best, and there have been many bests, this genre centers on a contemporary setting, realistic treatment, and a well-rounded central character whose experience is set firmly in the kind of world the reader lives through daily.

The protagonist (central character) is someone who thinks, reacts, puzzles, questions the world around and encounters the kinds of people that any of us might meet on the street, in the classroom, or anywhere in the world any day of our lives.

The sorts of problems a character may be forced to confront range through alienation, handicap, sex, drugs, alcohol, overweight, divorce, physical or psychological abuse—in other words, any conflict in which real human beings find themselves.

Obviously, not every young person is involved in situations of great dramatic proportions, but the not-so-easy process of growing up, making decisions, discovering self can provide material for this kind of book. The point is that the central character and the reader grow in some way in the course of the story. The narrative may not end happily, but it must end as a result of choices made by the protagonist.

Some novels typical of the genre are *Home Before Dark* (Bridgers), *A Day No Pigs Would Die* (Peck), *Are You There God? It's Me, Margaret* (Blume), *Bonnie Jo, Go Home* (Eyerly), *The Chocolate War* (Cormier), *The Divorce Express* (Danziger), *Abby, My Love* (Hadley Irwin).

Mysteries

A good mystery is fun to read and difficult to write. You must be a skilled and logical plotter to attempt one because the rules have long been established, and while you may work in innovations, your reader will be disappointed if you stray too far.

Generally speaking, the story revolves around a death, either deliberate or accidental, but violence in a YA mystery is not exploited as much as it might be in an adult novel. The game plays itself out either in a search for a perpetrator or, in the case of Lois Duncan's *I Know What You Did Last Summer,* a group of teenagers involved in a hit-and-run accident who are being sought by an avenger. Either way you set up the game, fast action and suspense are essential, sometimes at the expense of characterization.

Variations on the basic mystery characteristics may include humor: *From the Mixed-up Files of Mrs. Basil E. Frankweiler* (Konigsburg), fantasy: *The Young Unicorns* (L'Engle), or history: *The House of Dies Drear* (Hamilton). Perhaps one of the best known writers of YA mysteries is Jay Bennett. His stories *The Long Black Coat* and *The Dangling Witness* were Edgar Award winning books in 1973 and 1974.

Myth, Fantasy

Adolescents are avid readers of science fiction and fantasy, perhaps because of the enchantment they were once offered in fairy tales or perhaps because of the escape from "reality" such books provide. In this genre, the reader is transported forward or backward in time or is involved with a world where magic still reigns.

The appeal of fantasy is evident not only in literature but in the popularity of fantasy games such as *Dungeons and Dragons.* Inextricably mixed with the elements of mythology, the genre follows conventions that date back to the oral traditions of antiquity.

The idea of the quest undertaken by an innocent, aided often by an older, wiser person, perhaps a magician or a sorceress, is at the heart of fantasy. The world through which the protagonist moves is usually involved in a struggle between good and evil and is inhabited by creatures such as elves, dragons, ghosts, gnomes, and talking animals. It is a world in which danger lurks in many forms, where true friends are put to the test, where runes and magic talismans are keys to the accomplishment of the quest.

Quite often the literary quality of such writing is outstanding; the genre lends itself to symbolism, richness of language, to philosophic comment and to poetic vision. Although stories are often based on well-known legends such as Arthurian material, many are entirely new creations that owe nothing but conventions to the past.

For excellent examples try *The Dark Is Rising* or *The Grey King* (Cooper), *Dragonsong* (McCaffrey), *The Last Enchantment* (Stewart), *The Farthest Shore* (LeGuin), *Taran Wanderer* (Alexander).

Science Fiction

Science fiction has come a long way since the comic strip travels of Flash Gordon, but it never seems to lose readership. The genre offers protagonists who depend on intelligence as well as luck, frontiers that have yet to be tamed, endless worlds to explore with excitement, danger, and triumph on almost every page.

Science fiction is not limited to the logistics of space flight, or the invention of new kinds of lethal weapons, or invasion of the earth by alien life forms. The best SF writers, and there are many of them, create worlds which, while different from our own, are consistent with their own laws of science, morality, politics, justice. The only real suspension of disbelief necessary occurs during the amount of time it takes to open the book and begin reading.

One of the pleasures and challenges in writing science fiction is that it allows you freedom to examine our own contemporary world from a new perspective, to speculate on what aspects of humanity will be perpetuated and what may change them, and to explore utopian or antiutopian civilizations.

While not formulaic, this genre often is based on certain shared characteristics—a space voyage, encounters with different, though long-established cultures, an examination, either overt or implied, of problems that confront us now on planet Earth—the threat of nuclear war, overpopulation, damage to the ecology.

A sample of fine science fiction writers whose audience includes both young and adult readers would have to mention Isaac Asimov, Ray Bradbury, Arthur C. Clarke, Robert Heinlein, Ursula Le Guin, Anne McCaffery, and Andre Norton.

The Adventure Story

Pit a likeable protagonist against seemingly insurmountable obstacles or unsavory characters in a setting where nature too becomes an adversary and you have the ingredients for an adventure story. Whatever occurs, whatever the adventures or challenges—treks through jungles, storms at sea, rescues from floods, bravery in the face of catastrophe—the adventure must be one that young readers can believe could really happen, even if the story is set in another era.

The adventure story is full of action from the first page on, drawing the reader into the fast-paced plot which can employ surprises and heaped-on complications that often plunge the protagonist into even more jeopardy. The plot moves steadily on to its logical conclusion, omitting long descriptive passages and reflective monologues by the main character. Usually the plot is based on the need or the desire of the protagonist to achieve something. Of course, obstacles stand in the way, but the goal is achieved through the efforts of the protagonists themselves.

Characters in adventure novels must be completely believable, appearing as real living people in the reader's mind, not as stereotyped clones. Often the protagonist has a sidekick, either an animal or a loyal friend, and perhaps, lurking near, is a wise older person who acts as a mentor. Here the rule of "show, don't tell" is most applicable. Readers must learn the attributes of the protagonist through actions and words so that they can decide for themselves the kind of person who is engaged in the particular adventure. Some fine adventure stories for young adults include *Snowbound* by Harry Mazer, *Through a Brief Darkness* by Richard Peck and *Island of the Blue Dolphins* by Scott O'Dell.

Sports and Career Stories

Two types of books that were enormously popular in the 1940s and 1950s have maintained an audience in the 1980s, but have changed in their presentation of theme. Early sports stories were usually aimed at the male reader and centered on protagonists who eventually performed almost superhuman feats on the playing field in a sort of Horatio Alger plot. The hero, almost always male, was red-blooded, clean-cut, and a winner.

Today, the emphasis is on more realistic protagonists who have human weaknesses and faults, who may fail to reach a championship, but who manage to learn and grow along the way. Women athletes are slowly emerging as central characters in young adult books. Although relatively few books have been published so far, the trend is sure to pick up in the future.

Career books have followed a pattern similar to sports stories in that the emphasis is on a realistic approach to choosing and pursuing a career, rather than upon a rose-colored depiction of its nobility. Although nonfiction books about professions are probably in greater demand, there is still room for quality fiction.

Some examples of sports stories are *The Contender* (Robert Lipsyte), *High and Outside* (Linnea A. Due), *Fox Running* (R.R. Knudson). Career books include *Up the Down Staircase* (Bel Kaufman), *Fisherman's Choice* (Elsa Pedersen), *Max's Wonderful Delicatessen* (Winifred Madison).

Ethnic Cross-Cultural Books

Though not genres in themselves because of the wide range of subject matter and treatment, ethnic cross-cultural books form an important and needed addition to YA literature. For much too long, and in too many ways, the concerns, heritage, and problems of ethnicity have remained unexplored, or if treated, have been sensationalized or stereotyped. Fortunately, though slowly, the richness and diversity of the different cultures in America are being explored by a growing number of writers, some of whom write from their own ethnic heritage, some of whom, through research, imagination and caring, write from cross-cultural perspectives.

Whether a book is historical or contemporary, a problem novel or a biography, the important things to emphasize are accuracy and realism. The differences in culture as well as the commonality of experience are what make these books a valuable asset to YA literature. You must avoid the temptation to romanticize or moralize, always striving for the reality as opposed to the commonly held myth or stereotype.

For example, if you are Caucasian writing about a Native American, you must be aware of the significance and connotation of such details as colors, numbers, rituals, and metaphors. If you are a Native American aware of your heritage, you have the advantage of first-hand knowledge.

Language becomes a problem in this type of novel. You must strive to catch the speech rhythms rather than simply relying on dialect. If you do not belong to the ethnic group about which you want to write, you must be careful not to let culturally ingrained attitudes and misunderstanding creep in by way of hidden inferences. There is no room for knee-jerk liberals in cross-cultural writing. There is only room for honesty.

How exciting and enriching it will be for Young Adult Literature when the boat people, the mountain Mungs, and the Cambodian refugees find their own voices and write of their experiences, their heritage, and their culture.

A few of the books that you might read are *Bury My Heart at Wounded Knee* (Brown), *Executive Order 9066* (Conrat), *M. C. Higgins the Great* (Hamilton), *I Know Why the Caged Bird Sings* (Angelou), *My Name is Asher Lev* (Potok), *I Be Somebody* (Hadley Irwin), *Farewell to Manzanar* (Wakatuski), *Eyes of Darkness* (Jamake Highwater).

Historical Romance

This classification may seem ambiguous or paradoxical or just plain confusing, still it's useful because it describes a kind of book that has been popular with both adults and young readers for a long time. Romance in its broader definition promises a look at places, real places, removed in time or place. The reader expects adventure, excitement, and a certain amount of suspense, but also assumes that historical setting and events will be accurate.

This genre offers the opportunity to make moments of history come alive for the teenage reader. Part of the fun in writing an historical romance is that while the framework of your story may be factual, the specific events, as well as the characters, may be a mix of fact and fiction.

Research is important because of the need for accuracy in everything from clothing to customs to transportation to the popular culture of the period. Knowledgeable readers will scoff at anachronisms. The illusion of reality is created by paying attention to the specific detail, and those details allow you to evoke a particular era without constantly referring to dates.

Although the need for accuracy is supreme, you must not become so caught in historical truth that you forget what is equally important—the need to create a compelling story peopled with characters with whom the young reader can relate. For the writer, it's a balancing act without a net, but one that can be as exciting to accomplish as it is to watch.

In the historical romance, you must be careful not to attempt to cover too much history. A "slice" of the event is much easier to manage for the beginning writer and more palatable for the young reader. For example, the authors of *Until We Reach the Valley* (Avon: Reida Irwin) wished to portray a young Welsh girl on the Mormon Handcart Expedition across Iowa to Salt Lake, Utah. To cover the entire journey would be difficult for the authors and boring to the reader. Instead, the authors picked up the story when the central character arrived at the camp in Iowa where they would stay and build the wooden handcarts. The story ends at the Missouri River as the immigrants prepare for the next leg of the journey. A sampling of the Mormon trek was enough history upon which to build the plot.

If you are interested in historical romance, you might like to read *The Massacre At Fall Creek* (West), *Kate Ryder* (Burton), *We Are Mesquakie, We Are One* (Hadley Irwin), *Bargain Bride* (Lampman), *Blood Feud* (Sutcliff), *The King Must Die* (Renault).

Teenage Romances

A memory from the fifties has become news in the eighties. Teen romances are booming at the bookstores, moving into libraries, and providing entertainment for an entire generation of young adults. In many ways these books echo the adult romances that have appealed to millions of older readers. Spectacular success of the genre makes them impossible to ignore.

These are the books which are written *for* girls ten to sixteen and *about* that age group and are the books that girls choose to read not on the recommendations of teachers, parents, or librarians, but on the basis of their own taste and on the advice of friends. While adults debate the effect of romances on the attitudes and future reading choices of young adults, girls buy and read them by the million. Between 1981 and 1985, Bantam's "Sweet Dreams" series sold more than 18,700,000 copies. And there are dozens of series.

Although teen romances are devoured by millions of young girl readers, they have met with mixed reviews. They have been praised by some, deplored by others.

Some authors of young adult books were more specific. S. E. Hinton, who wrote her best-selling novel, *The Outsiders,* in 1967 as a reaction to the romances of an earlier generation, is quoted as saying, "Romances foster in young girls a feeling that they don't have an identity unless they have a boy. It's a backlash. Maybe the young adult books went too far in becoming problem books. There's so much insecurity in the world today, and the romances say that if you have a boyfriend, you'll be okay."

Robert Cormier, author of *The Chocolate War,* is still more precise: "The young adult field has taken such great strides in the last few years, dealing with topics like racism, homosexuality, old taboos, social issues, that it's too bad to see this great step be so much diminished by the influx of these bland teenage romances. But I'd rather see kids reading—even reading romances—than playing video games."

What are these books? What is their appeal? Who reads them? The audience is primarily made up of girls, many of whom consume between six and ten books each month, not such a difficult feat when you consider that a book can usually be read in about two hours. As to why the romances are so popular, the answer seems simple—a purely enjoyable read, no difficult problems, a predictably happy ending, and a cast of clean characters with whom the reader can easily identify.

The conventions of the genre are simple: a central character between the age of fourteen and seventeen, a relatively small cast of characters, a problem dealing with popularity or the lack of it, the right boy, success in becoming a cheerleader or the equivalent. The basic notion is that though the process of growing up may bring momentary difficulties, the teen years are mostly good, clean fun. Escape literature has always been popular; in that sense, these books are no different from thousands of their predecessors.

Although not confronting decisions about drugs, alcohol, sex, suicide, abuse, or any of the other situations that are part of too many teenagers' real lives, the books do explore the interests and concerns of young readers in an optimistic way.

Romance series employ the same conventions as the individual romance except that in the series, characters appear again in book after book, utilizing basically the same setting, the principle upon which successful TV soap operas are built. The formula works.

Fortunately for the would-be writer, the formula seems to have infinite variations, allowing you to move from "how to get a boy" stories to movement through time via computers (Avon's *Swept Away* series). If you are interested in writing romances, you really must become totally familiar with the market and with the characteristics of the particular series in which you feel you could succeed. While writing them is not as easy as it looks from a sample reading, there are some simple rules:

1. They must be clean—squeaky clean.
2. They must focus on the travails of teenage girls.
3. They must have a romantic interest that is all-consuming, but never consummated.
4. They must have a fast-moving, if not predictable, plot.

Most romance publishers have information sheets or guidelines that describe their line and define their particular needs. These may be had for the asking, but be sure to enclose a stamped, self-addressed envelope with your request.

If you can't wait for this material to arrive, you can begin by reading at least one book from each of the many publishers. Each has slightly different requirements. Pick the series you want to write for and study several of those books as carefully as you would if you were studying for a college entrance examination, outlining at least one of the books in detail. You may want to look at *Sweet Dreams* (Bantam), *Cheerleaders* (Scholastic), *Sweet Valley High* (Bantam), *Dream Girls* (Archway). Incidentally, don't overlook the ubiquitous Nancy Drew. The reemergence recently of an updated series of Nancy Drew, Tom Swift, Hardy Boys, and even the Bobbsey Twins proves that certain fictional characters, unlike old soldiers, neither die nor fade away. If you are adept at plotting a lively mystery or an engaging escapade, these series may be for you.

How long these teenage romances and series books will continue to find favor with the young is impossible to predict. Sometimes the very intensity of the reception of something new, whether in the form of books, clothing, music, or kinds of amusement, contributes to an early demise.

AFTER ALL, THE CHOICE IS YOURS

There are as many kinds of books as there are people, as many as the human mind can imagine—stories that center on animals, sports, careers, biographies; there are comedies, tragedies, satires, and probably a whole new direction that we have yet to discover. You write and we write because we have a story to tell that we find exciting and impelling and worth the time and work it will take to find its way to the printed page. Whatever you want to write, whatever genre you choose, whatever it is that you want to share, you must understand the markets, and you must understand your reader.

The genre you choose for your story will be dictated by at least three considerations: the basic ingredients of your plot—that is, what the book is actually about; its similarity to the kind of story you, yourself, like to read; and your possession of the specialized knowledge that a particular sort of story requires. Don't embark on a story about a teenage hacker unless you are a computer whiz yourself. Don't start a romance if you've never been in love. In other words, the field is wide open, and the choice *is* yours.

• three •

WHO'S YOUR READER AND WHO ARE YOU?

———◆———

One morning the daughter of one of the authors announced to her mother in tragic tones that when a child was twelve years old—her age—she was "in the midst."

Her mother politely inquired, "In what way?"

"She is in the midst," the child pontificated, "because she has one foot in the world of childhood and the other foot in the adult world, and most of the time she does not know which way to go."

True, thought her mother, then. She thinks so still. In fact, "in the midst," and its corollary "not knowing which way to go," might be a definition of adolescence itself.

It is this child who is the prototypical reader of Young Adult novels: informed and impressionable, wise beyond years lived, in some ways, and as abysmally ignorant in others, as easily swayed by peers as a blade of grass and yet able to stand rock-solid against parents on such subjects as dress, companions, or length of hair.

A fourteen-year-old girl on one day can go forth to shop with one of her friends, wearing lipstick, eye shadow, blusher, and mascara, and the next day wear dirty jeans and sneakers and play baseball in the park with her kid brother and his friends.

A boy can wear clothes so disreputable his parents will not

claim him and still appear on Sunday in his surplice looking like an angel and singing his heart out.

Kids also come in different colors and different backgrounds. The day has long since gone when it was assumed that all young people lived in white suburbs, where Daddy earned the living and Mommy stayed home and took care of the house and the kiddies.

Now we know better. Some kids live in substandard housing and may not have enough to eat. Sometimes Daddies stay home and Mommies go to work. Sometimes there isn't a daddy at all or a mother either.

CULTURAL EXCHANGE

The United States from its earliest beginnings has not only been the melting pot of the world but continues to absorb people from far lands and different cultures. In a nation of roughly 230 million people, 27 million are black. More than 14½ million are of Hispanic descent and three and a half million have forebears coming from—or having themselves recently come from—Japan, China and Southeastern Asia, the latter including Vietnamese, Koreans, and Laotians. Numerically few but culturally important, are Indians descended from those Native Americans whose land this once was. All of these cultures include children who in time will turn toward Young Adult books.

Kids' economic backgrounds vary even more than their color and country of origin. They come from families living below the poverty level, from families skirting it, and from those whose upward mobility increases until they not only become rich but very rich indeed. Many of today's children are latchkey children. Some of them come from broken homes and have witnessed the causes: alcoholism, unfaithfulness, chemical dependency, or abuse in one form or another.

A social worker tells of a call she made on a young welfare family. In the course of the interview, when the mother showed a recent vaccination which had turned raw and ugly, a small child standing nearby piped up and said, "Daddy did that."

The following little story is excerpted from a letter written

24

to one of the authors by a fourteen-year-old girl, a student in a transitional school, a drop-in school for drop-outs and other young people expelled from the regular school system. The letter begins

> ...maybe you can find time to read my story. It is called *Sister, Sister, Mother*. It is about this girl who couldn't handle things in her home. She feels the only way out is by killing herself. Her Mom never talks to the girl. Her sister beats her up all the time and I really would be honored if you could find the time to read it.

Sister, Sister, Mother

Once upon a time there was a girl who could not handle things in her home. She was cold and lonely. Her Mom never talked to her. The girl's sister beat her up all the time and one day the girl got tired of it all and wanted to end her life. She took thirteen sleeping pills. The girl realized what she had done and she cried.

She fell on the floor crying. And she put her hands together and she raised her head up to the sky and said, "God, I know I did wrong. Please don't let me die."

She really did not know what she was doing. She went and locked all the doors and put the chain on them. She was real tired by this time. She lay on the bed in the front room. The house was very small.

Three hours later her Mom came home and she tried to open the door but the chain was on. She screamed at the girl.

The girl was real drowsy but got the door open. Her mother asked questions like if anyone called. The girl was so out of it she said, "Daddy," but her dad was dead. Then her Mom knew something was wrong with the girl, but what? She went to the cabinet to get her pills from the doctor's office, but they were gone.

She said to the girl, "Where are my pills?"

The girl answered real slow, "I took them."

The girl's Mom called an ambulance. The girl was so bad they had to work on her in the house. They stuck IV needles in her arm and her Mom stood with a sad look on her face watching. And the girl could see the look on her face and the look she saw made her feel like she was in a whole new world. The feeling she had, she never had before.

The feeling was love, something she never dreamed she could have.

The next day she awoke and her Mom suddenly asked, "Why did you do this?" and started screaming. The girl could not do anything but stare. Her Mom said, "You did this for attention" and then walked right out the door. The girl was in a state of shock and to herself she was saying, "That's wrong," but she was so cold inside, she couldn't cry any more. She was all cried out. Her Mom walked back in and said, "Baby."

It was very quiet. They were in a warm embrace and the girl said, "Mom, I'm sorry." And her Mom said, "It is all right."

They had counseling sessions and her sister and her got along real well instead of fighting. They sat down and they talked about it. The girl was so pleased that everything was so nice, she would never try killing herself again. And they lived happy ever after.

The End of Part I

Part II was never written. The author of *Sister, Sister, Mother* has since dropped out of school and her whereabouts are unknown.

Although all adolescents certainly do not spring from such backgrounds but rather are members of a happy and supportive family, they know a lot, too. Sex and violence are all around and depicted daily in movies, on TV, and in magazines that seldom are kept under the counter.

Even so, such kids want to know more. Particularly, they like to read about kids older than themselves, thus giving themselves a taste of what is out there waiting for them. Though they may be too young to date, and have not yet had any "moves" made on them—"moves" being today's vernacular for yesterday's "making out" and day-before-yesterday's "necking"—they are vicariously thrilled reading about it. Many young people, though immune to pressure from their peers to smoke pot, join gangs, drink, or become involved with drugs, want to know what it's "like." The fact can be attested to by the continued popularity of such books as S. E. Hinton's *The Outsiders, Rumblefish,* and *That Was Then, This Is Now.*

THE MORE THINGS CHANGE, THE MORE . . .

Still, all is not doom and gloom. In a survey of 600 teenagers from six states, researchers from Southern Illinois University discovered that for high school boys "making the grade on the playing field" was top priority. For girls, it was being in the "right clique." For both boys and girls, other attributes for popularity, though not placed in the same order of importance, were "coming from the right family," "having a nice car," "being a leader in activities," and "being a cheerleader."

Probably the only cheering thing about these figures is that they do not differ materially from a similar survey taken ten years previously, nor from one fifteen years before that. "The more things change, the more they remain the same" still holds true and you will be safe in using these familiar ingredients of teenage noveldom if you can only figure how to do it in a new and interesting way. A cliché is a cliché whether a plot or a too familiar phrase.

BOY READERS VS. GIRL READERS

Many librarians who work with children believe that while girls will read a so-called boy's book—one in which the principal character and most of the other characters are boys—boys are much less apt to read a "girl's book." Boys, they say, would not touch a book like Judy Blume's *Forever*. Perhaps not "touch," say others who are more observant, but read them on the sly. A librarian who is the mother of a fourteen-year-old boy says her son doesn't bother putting a false cover on his sister's books when he borrows them; then she adds, "But that kid would read anything." As the gender gap diminishes, however, labels such as "boy's books" and "girl's books" may tend to disappear.

Librarians are more apt to agree that, as teenagers, girls read more than boys. Certainly, there are more books for them to choose from on the shelves of major-chain book stores such as B. Dalton and Waldenbooks, where there are dozens of titles of girl's books for every one or two for boys. Girls also tend to buy books by their favorite authors, exchange them with friends and read them over and over. It is not unusual for such young teens to have an overnight reading party.

Although there are no concise figures to prove that hardcover books for girls have a better chance of being published than those for boys, it *is* true when they are paperback "originals." The real winner, of course, is the author who manages to write a book in which the boy and the girl are equally interesting and the problem is one in which both are concerned. Richard Peck is an author who succeeds with *Remembering the Good Times*.

But no matter who the reader, it is an undeniable fact that the reading habits for both sexes have changed since the advent of what Barbara Tuchman calls "the easier alternative." There is not only less time for reading, but less need. Passive absorption of knowledge, via computer or TV screen, has become so common we have to remind ourselves that at one time reading was not taught. It was learned. Tuchman, in a lecture given at the Library of Congress, reminds us that years ago, it was not uncommon for very young children to be reading all kinds of books and memorizing reams of poetry. When he was three, Jonathan Swift was reading the Bible, and Dr. Johnson, the *Book of Common Prayer*. Lord Byron read constantly from the age of five, and the most voracious reader of them all was Thomas Babbington Macauley, who literally never stopped reading. Whatever he was doing, he had a book in his hand and died in his library with a book in his lap.

In today's schools, remedial reading courses are the norm, not the exception. Bright kids, invariably good readers, are siphoned off into classes that are termed "Talented and Gifted." This, however, leaves us with a lot of kids in between.

SO WHO *IS* YOUR READER?

Bear in mind with every word you write that there is no such thing as a "typical" teenager. Your readers are not a faceless conglomerate of kids, but young people who come from every economic and racial background.

Some are boys and some are girls. Some like to read and will stay with you while you get your novel underway. They are patient, for they know they have a good read ahead. Others whose attention span is short or for whom reading is a chore will require every trick you have in your bag to keep them with you to the end. But all of them—boy or girl, bright or slow, reader or nonreader—will be grateful if you write a book they can't put down. In this, they are no different from adults who gobble up the stories of Dick Francis and Robert Parker and keep authors like Robert Ludlum and Judith Krantz at the top of the *New York Times* Best Seller lists week after week.

It is helpful to post photographs of kids like those for whom you're writing at eye level just above your typewriter. If you give them a chance, they will "talk" to you.

Feelers

With these pictures before you, you are ready to tackle the other half of the problem: how to get through to this reader who is probably ten to fifty years younger than you are. If you are wondering if it is even possible to touch the emotional springs of those so young, the cheering answer is "yes." Regardless of your years, the most reliable source of accurate information is yourself. This will continue to be true throughout your writing life. The experiences of childhood and growing up, like the miraculous pitcher of Greek mythology that never became empty, will never be depleted no matter how much you call upon them.

On school visits the authors of this book have been asked many times the question: "How come you know how we kids feel and act when . . ." Here the questioners stumble a little because they are basically polite, ". . .when you, you know, you are really so . . . well . . . old."

Sometimes, we reply with a story about a friend's three-year-old granddaughter who came crying into the house one day saying her "feelers" had been hurt by the little boy next door; then we continue that no matter how *old* one is, one's "feelers" do not change. Whether one is the last kid chosen by the captains on the school playground as they take turns choosing their teams, or the grown man or woman who always sits alone in church or is left out when the neighbors plan a party, the hurt is never forgotten.

Pleasures also remain as lovely memories—the first kiss, how it feels to be in love. When you call forth the bitter and sweet memories of your youth, you will most likely find them—the "feelers," that is—as fresh as they were when you first experienced them.

Should these memories, however, have dried up or be painful ones you do not want to recall, you can safely depend on your feelings as an adult. Being rejected feels the same whether one is fifteen or fifty. Being ridiculed or whispered about behind your back is every bit as painful at forty as at fourteen. Being alone in the house at night when the stairs creak and a door into your bedroom slowly opens is as terrifying when you are old as when you are young.

Deep Thinking

Another source of surprise is the subconscious. Although most literary people know they have one, they don't spend a lot of time thinking about it. But if you, the author, learn to drop a plumb line into its depths, very likely you will find you have gained new insights into the life of your characters. Sometimes this will enable you to fill in a "black hole" similar to one of those voids that appear in outer space and, quite as unaccountably, turn up in a novel. Such material will add authenticity to the lives of the young people you write about.

The process demands what we call "deep thinking." What it brings to the surface will be something that could have come only from you. It demands practice. Start with an early memory. It may be something that actually happened to you or it may be something implanted in your mind by constant telling and retelling of the event by parent or relative. No matter. The essence of the experience is still there and it is up to you to dredge it out.

For instance, when you were quite small do you remember the panic you felt when you were separated from your family at the State Fair? The airport in a strange city? Do you recall the terror that overcame you that dark night when you were out collecting for your newspaper route and you heard footsteps behind you, stopping when you stopped, their pace increasing when you increased yours? Do you remember pulses you never knew you had that started pounding when the new boy across the street carried out the garbage every night? Remember the thoughts that flashed through your mind the night you went skinny-dipping in the gravel pit and almost drowned when that cramp hit you?

You may not recreate any of these scenes in your novel—though it is very likely you might—but the feelings you had will serve you well when they are translated into situations of your own making.

Alfred Hitchcock's understanding of fear enabled him to produce films that kept movie-goers rigid in their seats. Fear had been ingrained in him as a child of five when his father, a green-grocer in London, sent him for some unexplained reason to the police station with a note. For an even more inexplicable reason, the Chief of Police locked the child up in a cell, keeping him there five minutes before releasing him with the playful threat, "That's what we do to bad little boys." Hitchcock is said never to have forgotten the experience, and all his life remained a frightened man, fearful of heights, closed spaces, small children, figures of authority, and so fearful of arrest he never drove a car.

Judy Blume, probably more than any other popular author, has found the inspiration for novel after novel by her ability to "get through" to the young reader by delving deep into memories of her own childhood and adolescence. A grade school experience in Florida where her family, because of a brother's poor health, had moved for the winter—only her dentist father remained behind in Elizabeth, New Jersey—eventually became the source of *Starring Sally J. Freedman As Herself*. Worries about menstruation, her fear that she would be the last in her group to "get" it, resulted in the now almost classic book of adolescence, *Are You There God? It's Me, Margaret*.

Other snatches of actual happenings appear here and there in Blume's other books. Remember the scene in *Then Again, Maybe I Won't* where Tony Miglione and his pals leave a tip for the waitress in the bottom of an empty milkshake glass? Blume didn't invent it. As a teenager, she and a friend played the same trick on a waitress in a soda shop in downtown Elizabeth. She did

31

not have to go far back into the past to find the inspiration for *Blubber*, a fat girl in her daughter's class at school whom the other kids teased unmercifully. A teenager with scoliosis (curvature of the spine) who lived in Blume's neighborhood became the inspiration for *Deenie*. Total involvement with the story came from watching kids like Deenie being fitted for body braces in the hospital.

JUST REMEMBER . . .

Your audience, male or female, are young adults who want to be entertained, enlightened, and excited by the words you put on the page. They are probably little different from the person you once were, except in superficial ways. Although an intellectual awareness of life is important in the process of crafting a story, your "feelers" and your memories of your own reactions to growing up can be just as valuable to you. Though they may be submerged or almost forgotten, they are still there.

Dig for them. Make use of them. Get to know the teenager you were. Knowing that plus understanding your audience will help ensure your success as a writer.

• four •

BEFORE YOU TOUCH THE KEYS

---◆---

Few things in life are as easy as NOT writing the book that you've always intended to begin. One of the best excuses is that you don't have in mind an entire story line complete with characters and dialogue just waiting to spring to life on the page. If you hope for that kind of magic, chances are the book will never be written. Writing, unlike preparing instant soup mix, is not a matter of just adding water and heating. You may have the basic ingredients at hand, but good writing takes thought and preparation to begin the process.

A blank sheet of paper in the typewriter is always intimidating, but at the outset of an unwritten novel, it is terrifying. Where in the world will those 40,000 words come from? How in the world can you manage to fill almost 200 pages of empty paper? How do you begin the process of writing a book?

IDEA

Granted there are as many ways to write as there are writers; no one way is right for everyone, but here's something to consider. Simplistic as it sounds, a book starts with an idea, a random notion that attracts, intrigues, creates questions—something worth the time and agony and frustration that are inevitable in the process of writing.

Someone has said that an idea has some of the mysterious quality of an atoll or island that suddenly appears in a spot where ancient charts showed nothing but deep blue sea. Mysterious? Not if you think of the countless, unseen coral builders working below the surface of the sea. Not if you think of an idea being the final result of a long series of unseen idea-building processes which go on beneath the surface of the conscious mind. It is this unseen building process that has sparked many of the world's great inventions.

Where does that idea come from? Better to ask how one can avoid ideas. They are all around, everywhere, everyday. Most of them are no more dramatic than the ubiquitous phrase, "Have a good day." Come to think of it, that *is* a good idea. It could go in a dozen different directions and result in a dozen different books.

A well-known and prize-winning author of young adult books said rather pettishly that when people asked her, as they were always doing, where she got her ideas, she just turned the tables on them and asked them where they got *their* ideas. The implication was that she thought such questions stupid. Many authors, fortunately, don't mind being asked such questions because they know exactly where the idea arose. Sometimes, it is from something read in a newspaper or magazine, a personal experience or that of a friend, something heard or overheard. But whatever it is or whatever triggered it, a light goes on in the mind as it is pictured in comic strips: a little balloon rises above one's head bearing the word "IDEA!"

The Lilith Summer (Hadley Irwin) began with a newspaper photograph of an eighty-five-year-old woman who had just been told by a social worker that she could remain in her own home and not have to be moved to a care center. It was a picture of age and triumph. *We Are Mesquakie, We Are One* owes its birth to a footnote in an Iowa history book about the Mesquakie Indian tribe in the 1800s. The comment of a junior high girl, "He's NOT my boy friend. He's just a friend who happens to be a boy," ended up as *Moon and Me*.

Ideas are everywhere: in visual images, overheard conversations, visits to the local supermarket, talk shows on radio or television, even in the advice columns of newspapers. Nothing is wasted as far as a writer is concerned.

THE DARKER SIDE

Although ideas are everywhere, sometimes *the* idea that will start you on your way is elusive.

Should this be the case, a modified genealogy chart is not a bad place to begin. Who *are* you? Who are your parents? Where did they come from? If they or their parents were immigrants in the last century, what was their country of origin and why did they leave? What ambitions and ideals did they bring with them that have then been passed on to you? Or did you, somewhere along the line, reject them because of their grammar, or the way they dressed and the way they lived?

If you can find nothing in your family history that is unique, nothing that gives you particular insight into the condition of today's teenagers, you may look at your own immediate life and also find nothing there. But if you pause for a moment, the "light" comes on. The idea may lie in your very lack of uniqueness. Searching for your own identity—finding out "who you are"—to use today's vernacular—might become the theme of a novel that would appeal to hundreds of thousands of young teenagers who are searching for an identity of *their* own.

There are potential ideas in other sources and none are more fruitful than hobbies, sports, and special interests if they are looked at with a fresh eye. If you are a golfer, what about the caddy who carries your clubs and collapses one day on the course? Idea? Tennis? Handball? Swimming? Name almost any sport in which you excel or have a particular interest and you will find that the germ of an idea lies within. If yours are more passive pastimes, what about chess? Ham radio? Model airplane building? That electric train set you got as a kid and that over the years has grown so large the basement will hardly contain it? Clothes designing? Modeling? Any profession or job that is usually thought of as being "man's work," or conversely, "woman's work," in which you or someone you know has succeeded?

Are you a history buff? There is no richer field of exploration than that in our own country. Fine books have been written around little-known events. Are you an amateur ornithologist? Geologist? Philatelist? The "ists" go on and on.

Certainly not all lights that go on in the mind materialize into novels, but the good ones do not go away. They are filed in your mental computer until the time comes for them to be peopled with flesh and blood characters and become a novel. One author says that all of her ideas are the result of what her now-grown daughters, not unkindly, call "Mother's insatiable curiosity." Another author likens an idea to a snowball so small it can be held in one's hands, then gathering more snow as it rolls along.

It is uncanny how an idea, once lodged in the mind, does gather reinforcements. The idea for *See Dave Run* (Eyerly) came from a newspaper item. It told the story of a fifteen-year-old runaway who was picked up by police in a small midwestern town and was jailed until juvenile authorities could figure out what to do with him. The boy, left alone, used the drawstring from his nylon jacket as a noose and hanged himself. The author clipped the story, filed it, and as is customary with her home filing system (which she does not recommend) lost it. But she did not forget it.

Six months later an inch-long Associated Press story from somewhere in Texas reported a similar juvenile suicide. Over the next several years other such stories appeared from different quarters of the United States, reinforcing the original idea. All in all, five years elapsed from the time she read the first story until the day she sat down, named the characters, and plotted the novel. Of course she knew the ending before she started.

IDEA TO THEME

The first step, then, is the perception of what is there to be seen or heard. The second step is turning the idea into a theme or point that will control the direction and destiny of the book. The purpose of your writing will be to make this abstract concept or theme concrete through character, plot, and image.

A little girl explained *theme* best when she said it is what you remember about a book after you have forgotten who the characters were and what they did. You will not want your young reader to finish reading your story and say, "So what?" Thinking through your story with a theme or a point in mind will provide *meaning* to your book. Try to express your theme in a sentence, complete with subject and predicate, so that it expresses something *about* your subject.

Only the writer of a particular story knows what triggered the basic idea for a book, or *how* it turned into a theme that gave a clear direction to the writing. It's a personal and idiosyncratic process.

An example of idea to theme began *What About Grandma* (Hadley Irwin). A friend remarked, "I've been a daughter all my life and a mother half my life. When do I get to be me?" The idea that arose had to do with role playing. The theme that emerged became something like "Within a family, the roles of grandmother, mother, and daughter can be painful if love and understanding are forgotten."

No matter how the theme is expressed, it suggests what characters may emerge, what incidents may arise. It's important to remember that a novel is a matter of cause and effect: each cause results in certain effects; each effect creates new causes. In that sense, character and incident interact to produce plot, which illuminates theme. No one element of a novel is independent of the others.

In this way theme is revealed because it is implicit to the logic of the narrative. If it is made explicit at all, the overt statement may come through dialogue of one of the characters, never by you as the author any more than you would tell a joke and then explain the point. The story must speak for itself.

REPERCEPTION

If ideas have their roots in perception, and theme is clarification of that perception, the narrative itself arises from *reperception*. Without reperception, the same books would be written over and over again much to the dismay of authors, publishers, and readers. It all has to do with the way you look at things. For the Biblical Noah, that ungainly ark he was building was a way to literal salvation; to his neighbors it must have been an urban blight. Perhaps, when the deluge began, those same folk had a moment of reperception.

Reperception, or "epiphany" (for which term we owe James Joyce), is a time or a sudden flash of recognition, or perhaps better phrased, new cognition. What is actually there in the physical world, what has presumably always been there, is seen anew.

Just as this term can be applied to what exists in reality, it may also be descriptive of the new viewing of an abstraction. In either case, you step aside and look at an object aslant. The elements that you're viewing remain the same, but their arrangement, their meaning, may take on entirely different dimensions and connotations. If you've ever looked into a kaleidoscope, you'll understand what happens. Here, the only difference is that your own mind acts as a substitute for the glass mirror.

The results of an author's reperception appear *in* everything from imagery to figures of speech to the entire fictional world created in the pages of a book. Fiction is not the art of reproducing reality; it is the art of creating the *illusion* of reality, and that illusion springs from reperception.

Perhaps the most famous example is Proust's tasting madeleine and tea, which triggered the many-volumed *Remembrance of Things Past*. In an entirely different context, though the result of the same process, in Crane's *Red Badge of Courage,* the sun is described as a red wafer pasted on the sky. In Irving's *The World According to Garp* the notion of the Great Under-toad is the same kind of thing.

At base, then, reperception is another word for imagination or insight. Whether the act is willed or unconscious, it is the very heart of fiction. Without it, even the most polished writing will not stir the reader, will not touch the reader's heart.

Perhaps the most wonderful thing about reperception is that it allows writers to deal with the same themes, yet produce entirely different books. Both *Huckleberry Finn* and *Catcher in the Rye* show boys growing toward adulthood, yet each is distinct, individual. While a reperception of reality may give impetus to the concept upon which your story is based, it's also an ongoing process throughout the actual writing. It is the creation of something that has never before existed.

WHAT IF?

Writing fiction means venturing into the world of "what if?" The words themselves demand an answer to their question, and, in turn, the answer is an imaginative act.

The overheard bit of conversation, "He's just a friend who happens to be a boy," was the basis of *Moon and Me* (Hadley Irwin). A girl said it, but surely not as the start of something she would eventually understand; rather it was a conclusion she had come to.

WHAT IF that "she" is the central character and the book concerns situations that lead to that understanding? WHAT IF she is a sophomore in high school? That's a nice, in-between, transitional sort of time. WHAT IF she is in a new school, she never had a date, has a highly romanticized idea of what "boyfriend" means? Girls that age are often more interested in senior boys than in their classmates who have yet to grow tall and are still barely peering over the tops of their desks.

WHAT IF the one senior "she" is interested in is unaware of her existence? WHAT IF, however, another boy is fascinated by her even though he is in the eighth grade and the top of his head comes as high as her armpit? We already know the end of the story, what she is going to learn, but *how* will she learn? What will happen in the story? What is the story line?

Is it possible to write a book without knowing everything that will occur? Certainly it is. Once you've thought about the what if's, you'll have an idea of who your major characters are. What you need next is a setting and some notion of the length of time in which your story will take place.

Setting

Town, city, country, sun belt, Midwest, either of the coasts— choose the setting you know best. Choose a setting that you care about. Human relationships, problems, emotions are not tied to one spot on the map unless, of course, your central character *has* to be a native of Sri Lanka or the Isle of Wight in which case you have reason for a fascinating research trip.

While you must be accurate in your use of setting, you don't want to become so "regionalized" that your references will be incomprehensible to readers outside the particular area. An incident involving "walking beans" (walking along bean rows to weed them by hand), though clear enough in the Midwest, would not be understood by a reader in New York unless you stopped the action and spent valuable time in exposition—almost always a bad idea.

Nor do you want to rely on stereotypic settings—the high school prom in the gym, the drive-in restaurant, the local swimming pool. Of course, events may occur in any of those places, but as major settings they are as trite as the "malt shops" of the forties. Remember, too, that while you should be as familiar as possible with the settings you choose, your reader will not be interested in pages of description. Setting should appear as a part of the action and should contribute to the mood and the movement of the narrative. It should be made apparent through the perceptions of the characters, not through the voice of the author.

In establishing setting, time is as important as place. Whether your story is contemporary, historical, or futuristic, the details of life must be authentic. The artifacts, styles, and habits of the 1950s are quite different from those of the eighties or the years past 2,000—make sure they're either accurate or convincing. A single reference to a hair style or a way of dressing can indicate the era in which your book is set—thus saving paragraphs of exposition and explanation.

Still another aspect of time as part of setting is the question of how much fictional time your book will cover. Consider how long it might realistically take for your major character to encounter, understand, and solve a problem or a conflict. Think about what seasons of the year would offer activities in which your characters could be involved as part of their everyday lives. There are many techniques with which you can handle the passing of time (flashback for one), but you may find that in a first book, a short time is better; at least it's easier to handle.

All of those decisions have been made and still there is no complete story line! You may be the sort of writer who is comfortable only with a complete outline or who needs a cast of characters named, categorized, each with an entire biography typed out on file cards, ready for instant plug-in at the appropriate moment in the story. There's nothing wrong with that if it makes you comfortable, but there is another way. It is writing the first sentence of your book and remembering that your words are not engraved in stone.

Working Title

If you're foolish or brave enough to tell whoever will listen that you're writing a book, they won't believe it unless they find you at your typewriter or desk or whatever it is you write with or upon. A great deal of the process takes place in the mind before you ever touch the keys; thinking through is a quiet, lonely business.

At some time in the process, you may well want to come up with a working title. It may make the book idea real; it may fend off friendly and unfriendly questioners. It can work as a light from a distant house as you walk along a lonely road. It can keep you on track in your thinking and eventually in your writing. Thinking through your idea and theme and establishing a possible title may prevent you from wandering off your path.

Many writers, of course, prefer to wait until they've finished a first or even final draft to give a name to their work; they feel that a working title constrains their imagination and limits the direction of their story. For a first book, however, a title, even though it may never be used, gives the writer a sense of direction.

The title should give a hint of what your book is about and promise something to the young reader. It should be original, catchy, and state or imply some action or conflict. Think about stories or novels that you've read and loved. What were the titles—names, questions, quotations, or declarations? Did they pique your interest before you read and did they seem satisfactory when you'd finished the book? Remember *Call of the Wild, The Secret Garden, Catcher in the Rye, The Outsiders, The Cat Ate My Gym Suit, Pardon Me, You're Stepping On My Eyeballs*?

The working title may never become the actual title, but it can be a reassuring beginning. The real work lies ahead on the day you sit down to create a world from your own imagination, but you may become aware that much as you thought you knew about your subject there is still more to learn before the actual writing begins.

Research

The foundation of a Young Adult novel or any piece of fiction is careful research of your idea. A writer's knowledge is like an iceberg: only the tip of the mass hidden beneath the ocean surface is visible. Whether your story concerns the contemporary or the past or even the future, you may amass boxfuls of data for a novel of no more than 250 pages, yet the unused mass is a must if your story is to carry the ring of authenticity.

Research is fun; in fact, it can be so engrossing and addictive that you may put off writing the actual story. Writers tend to look inward rather than outward, but in doing research for a Young Adult novel you must learn to look outward, observing everything through the eyes of the characters in your story. In fact, a true researcher works with two sets of eyes: his own and his character's.

In researching material for *Kim/Kimi,* the authors took a first trip to Sacramento, California, as their character, Kim, would do in the story. Not only did they keep track of their own observations, but they were constantly asking themselves, "If I were Kimi, what would I notice?" Kimi was sixteen; the authors were many years her senior.

The process of research takes not only the author's but also the character's lack of knowledge into account. In other words, writers learn along with their characters. You and your character are exploring the world when you are engaged in research for a Young Adult novel. If you have a character who is growing up in 1885, that character is obviously aware of the time and setting, and in this case, the author has to catch up with the knowledge that the character already has. In either case, unless you have lived through it and remember it all, research is as necessary as typewriter ribbon.

Primary Sources

Firsthand experience is certainly the most authentic source of information for a writer, but many other such primary sources are available. Letters, diaries, and journals can provide not only factual data but emotional reaction, personal feelings, and private observations which can be a fine aid in character development. For one writer, a diary written by a teenager telling of an Indian raid on her log cabin provided an insight into the fears and dangers children faced in the early days of the nation. A writer's own diary from the teenage days can recapture the joys and sorrows of adolescence, and of course, your own journal of ideas can be a rich source of inspiration when the creative juices are running thin.

Trips to visit unfamiliar as well as familiar locales are most fruitful to observe specific details of setting, to listen to speech patterns, to soak up local color, and to experience the real world of your story. Don't just drop in. Stop. Look. Listen. A two-day attendance at an August Pow-Wow provided another facet of understanding of Native American culture. Hadley and Irwin were brought up short when they began to write the first paragraph of *I Be Somebody* and discovered they didn't know what kind of trees grew in Clearview, Oklahoma. A trip not only solved the problem, but several days spent in the area provided them with a visual memory of the town as well as a sense of its past. A visit to the town's cemetery revealed a large tombstone towering over the leading citizen's grave and enabled them to add a new family to the cast of characters for the story.

Some information may have to be obtained from individuals having specific knowledge of a particular subject. Though this may be contained in only a sentence or two in your book, it must be accurate. How does a fireman carry a child down a ladder from the window of a high building? For a scene in *The Seeing Summer* (Eyerly) it was necessary to know. A fireman at a neighborhood fire station, told the reason for the request, supplied a quick and cheerful answer. It appears in the book: "Then it was Carey's turn. Slung over the back of the fireman like a bag of flour, and with one of his strong arms around her, she was not afraid."

If you do not know the name of someone who has the information you need, it will be necessary to search out someone who does know. Readers will be quick to catch you up. Even the slightest altering of facts or faking information can damage your credibility.

Lois Horowitz in her book *A Writer's Guide to Research* suggests consulting professional journals and similar publications to locate names of interviewable experts one can phone or write to. She also recommends calling the public relations offices of companies that are concerned in one way or another with what you want to know. Universities and colleges are teeming with experts who usually are keen on their subject and willing to share. Do not hesitate to query your neighborhood pharmacist about drug information. Hospitals, vying with each other for business, have special departments dealing with everything from drug dependency to sleep disorders and are good sources of information, as are directors of botanical centers, zoos, art museums and science centers. The section of your local telephone book that deals with city, county, state, and federal offices is usually broken down so that every department can be located with ease.

For all interviews, there are a few simple rules. Identify yourself. If you have a specific job title, give it: "I am a teacher with the public schools here and I am writing a book about. . . ." or simply, "I am writing a novel for young people about. . . ." Make it clear that the interview will be brief and involve not more than fifteen or twenty minutes of the person's time. It is not likely you will be refused. Even busy people are flattered when they are viewed as experts. On the day of the interview, arrive promptly at the appointed time. Have the questions you want answered written out in as concise a form as possible. Take notes if need be, but do so as inconspicuously as you can. It is possible to scribble on a note pad without taking your eyes from the speaker's face. If answers are apt to be complex, take a tape recorder with you, but ask permission to use it. It is also wise to check on what your subject has told you by doing additional reading or interviews. Everyone has a tendency to fictionalize.

Secondary Sources

If you can't obtain all the information you need from primary sources, the public library or the nearest college or university library is bulging with secondary sources. What fun to spend a week or two as a library lounge-lizard. Don't hurry with your research. Remember, a writer is first a reader. Delve into whatever interests you. Be the curious one. Check the card files for more source books than you will ever have time to read. Search out magazine articles by using the *Readers' Guide to Periodical Literature*. Browse through the genealogy section of the reference department. Don't neglect the racks of masters and doctoral theses in a university library. Ask the library personnel for guidance. Not only will they help you search out books, but through interlibrary loans will procure from other libraries books not on their shelves. The cost is minimal, usually just the cost of mailing the material from its home base to your library and back again.

Old newspapers are available, usually for viewing on microfiches. These provide interesting background material on the events of the day, movies that were playing, weather, and politics. Even though the book you are writing does not depend on such specific information, sometimes even including bits and pieces adds richness to your novel.

Historical societies, museums, and courthouse records can all provide you with material in the form of old records and documents. It is also possible to receive through the mail printed material, not only from government and social agencies, but from private organizations on practically every subject imaginable: teenage pregnancy, drug abuse, social diseases, suicide, cancer, alcoholism, weight control. Such material can be passed on to your library after you have finished with it.

Organizing Your Findings

The efficient researcher meticulously records all data on note cards and files them, by subject, for easy reference. Some writers, however, scrawl notes and ideas on the back of a stray envelope, on table napkins, old letters, grocery lists, and toss them in whatever receptacle is handy. Then when the writing begins, this poor soul is forced to dig through the magpie nest of paper scraps to locate that perfectly super idea. Suffice to say that research is an individual matter. Whatever works for you is best, but somewhere—in a journal or diary or special notebook—you should have a place to jot down those ideas that come to you like gifts from the gods. How often you will say, "I'll have to remember that," but when you need just that very idea, you will find it has flown. Unless you have a photographic memory, write those ideas down—somewhere.

Plagiarism

Although with fiction there is little danger of plagiarism—that is following an original source too closely—you should be especially aware of such a practice if you are working on an historical novel. A good method to keep yourself honest is to copy the exact words from the original source, giving proper credit to the author, then learn to paraphrase. It is an art often neglected.

> *Original:* When Iowa grain fields wave golden in the August sun and corn tassles feather into yellow-green plumes, the Mesquakie Indians assemble on the Old Battleground for their annual powwow.
> *Paraphrase:* In August, the Mesquakies began to gather for their annual powwow on the Old Battleground.

The central idea of the information is common knowledge, but the particular words belong to the original author.

USING YOUR RESEARCH

Evidence of your thorough research should permeate your story, camouflaged so that young readers are not turned off by long passages of description and exposition (explanation). Weave your knowledge into action, setting, speech patterns, mannerisms, background, dress, idioms, so that readers will discover that they not only enjoyed your story, but learned as well.

Note how the author's research flows into the action of the story:

> He scuffed down the dirt road toward school. How come things had to fit? He could never get all those bits and pieces Aunt Spicy was talking about stuck together, like looking around now he could see a hawk circling overhead, and if he turned and looked back, he could see the timber climbing out of the valley and running up the side of Big Hill, and he knew Salt Creek lay beyond, but he couldn't see them all in one piece.

Research is a way of totally immersing yourself in a place and time so that when your characters appear, they are as familiar to you as your own family, and you can walk the streets of your fictionalized town as easily as if you had lived there all your life. You will be educating your young reader with your "bits and pieces" of research sprinkled into your story and you will be educating yourself as well.

Remember, however, you are doing research for a Young Adult novel, not for a high school term paper or a doctoral dissertation. You are looking not only for facts, you are looking for sensations, feelings, auras, atmosphere from which to create an imagined series of events called fiction. Historical fiction requires both the facts and the feelings, but one danger in writing this type of story is that facts often crowd out the pace of the plot. Whatever the case, relax after the period of intensive research to let the idea of your story and the facts of your research marinate before starting the actual writing of your story.

LOOK BEFORE YOU LEAP; THINK BEFORE YOU WRITE

Writing a novel is a time- and energy-consuming adventure, one that will test your patience and your staying power before you can finish that last page. There is no easy way of writing, but you can simplify the process a bit by giving yourself advance thinking time.

Whether you are planning a trip to the moon, a visit to the neighborhood supermarket, or a novel, preparation time is never wasted. Have the theme of the story clearly in mind, get to know your characters, do the necessary research, enjoy the discoveries you will make—then it's time to write!

five

IN THE BEGINNING

---◆---

The scene is a classroom in a midwestern city; the occasion, the first session of a class in Writing for Young Adults, sponsored by the Adult Education Department. In response to the teacher's question, "Do any of you have any particular problems?" a serious young man in the front row holds up his hand.

"I've this wonderful idea for a novel," he says, "but I don't know where to begin."

The speaker is one of eleven people who have paid a modest fee to learn, they hope, the secret of successful novel writing. They are of both sexes and of all ages: two women in their mid-sixties, a man in a Brooks Brothers suit, a city fireman, three high school English teachers, a man with a sunburned face who wears a seed-corn cap, an overdressed blonde who wants to write a sizzling romance for adults but thinks it might be easier to write for kids, a social worker, and a woman who later admits that she is there by mistake. She had thought she was signing up for a class in cake decorating, but confesses the class is so interesting she thought she would stay for a while.

"That's my question, too," says the man in the seed-corn cap, ". . . knowing where to begin."

Although other problems surface with dialogue, characterization, and plotting, all agree that where to start is all-important, particularly as no one in the class has yet begun to write.

Knowing where to begin is a problem faced by writers everywhere. Whether from a young person studying Creative Writing in college, working at a more advanced level in a university Writers' Workshop, or a lonely individual hunkered over a typewriter without even a correspondence course to follow, the plaint is the same. It is a problem faced not just by beginners but by long-time professionals and is compounded by the fact that the author has not decided from whose point of view the story is to be told.

DECISIONS! DECISIONS!

Writing is the process of making choices and one of the most important choices you will make concerns the point of view from which your story will be told. The result of your decision may move the novel smoothly from start to finish or it may stop you flat in the middle of a chapter and make you rethink the way in which your reader will respond to the narrative.

The term "point of view" in writing fiction has little in common with the term as it is used in casual conversation: "Oh, yes, I can understand your point of view." In a novel it has to do with the person who is living the story, and, in turn, conveying it to the reader, only secondarily with the biases, background, and perceptions of that particular person.

Perhaps the best way of understanding point of view is to start with the notion that when you write a story, you are creating a fictional world, one that has never existed before. It doesn't matter if the world you devise is filled with talking animals and little pink people or is one that more nearly resembles our own. In either case, the world springs from your imagination and experience, and you must allow your reader access to it. That access comes through point of view.

All-Seeing, All-Knowing Narrator

The omniscient point of view is an old and traditional one. It has been around ever since Homer and probably long before. It depends on the all-powerful writer's ability to move through time and space, in and out of characters' minds quite freely. You may, in the course of your story, skip through generations, move from New York to San Francisco within the space of one paragraph to the next or you may offer a scene in which we not only see and hear characters, but also know what each one is thinking.

This technique works to advantage in terms of the scope it gives the writer in the ability to contrast characters' reactions and psyches. It can be particularly effective in creating tension and excitement in an adventure story because the reader can see and understand developments that are not clear to the characters who are participating in the events. Though unrealistic at base, the method can work well if the story and characters are exciting enough to create the "suspension of disbelief." Done badly, it makes the reader more aware of author manipulation and can lead you, as author, into depending on coincidence rather than character for plot complications. The bigger danger is leap-frogging from one character's point of view to another in such an obvious way that the reality of the story is destroyed.

In many popular adult novels the leap-frogging danger is usually ignored by both writer and reader, because such leaps speed the story along, allow for numerous subplots, and hasten the next bedroom scene involving a different cast of characters. Most Young Adult books do not employ this technique, or if they do, it is used primarily for setting a scene or beginning a story. In the hands of an expert, the omniscient point of view creates a sense of atmosphere, then quickly and smoothly shifts direction into third person, focusing on just one central viewpoint character.

Ouida Sebestyen's lovely novel, *Words by Heart*, begins in exactly this way.

> Old Bullet had guessed they were going somewhere—Lena's folks—before they came out the door. He stood under the wagon like a spare horse, wagging hopefully. Ben Sill's family hadn't mingled much since they came from Scattercreek, where everyone was black, to this town where no one was. But tonight was a special night, Lena's night, when her Magic Mind was going to matter, not her skin.

As they were leaving, a firefly star winked out over the roof of the rent-house they had lived in that summer. Lena asked up at it, Is tonight when my whole life changes?

The Limited Narrator

Using a limited third-person viewpoint offers a greater sense of reality because it relates more nearly to actual human experience. You focus upon your central character and are free to offer the reader that character's thoughts, actions, reactions, even psychological hang-ups. We see the events of the story through his or her eyes and are limited only by what that character could know or guess about other people and circumstances that are part of the plot.

The particular problem here is that everything must be couched in the terms and language of that character. If your protagonist is fourteen, she cannot suddenly begin speaking in your thirty-five-year-old voice.

In *I Be Somebody* (Hadley Irwin) Rap is a black ten-year-old leaving Oklahoma for Canada in 1910. It is the first train ride of his life:

> Rap took the tin cup and started down the aisle. At first he didn't know what had happened. Maybe it was because he had been sitting at the window so long his legs had forgotten how to walk. He didn't think he'd ever sat still so long before, longer even than Mrs. Crumpton's study periods. He took one step and bumped into the seat across the aisle. He grabbed to steady himself, but was thrown against the opposite seat. It was like trying to swim upstream in Salt Creek. He zigzagged down the length of the car like one of the big Smolletts when he got too much home brew.

Notice that we are listening in on Rap's thoughts, yet there are no "he thoughts" interspersed as attributives. If you have firmly established your characters, then thoughts will be so natural to the reader that they don't need taglines such as "he thought" and "he felt." It also follows that everything else—descriptions, moments of action—will be seen and understood through Rap's perception. In other words, there is no consciousness of the author.

In this case, Rap is the central character, but the limited third-person point of view works equally well for a character who observes rather than directly participates in the major events that occur. The technique creates a certain distance from the action, and allows the character to comment, draw analogies, make judgments, and interpret actions and reactions.

I, The Narrator

First person point of view, often maligned because it *seems* so easy, can be most effective because it allows instant empathy of reader for character. Many of the problems in using the "I" are no more difficult to deal with than are those of the limited third-person "she" or "he." It becomes a matter of remembering the limits of what one character can know and the places where one character can be. The difficulty here is to reveal to the reader the necessary information or events that take place ouside the realm of the "I." One, if creative, can circumvent such problems through the use of conversations which the "I" hears or participates in, through remembered conversations, through the thoughts of the "I" and the more slippery technique of resorting to journals, diaries, or letters.

When the "I" is telling the story, character description and revelation may become a problem too. The author must reveal the "I" character through actions, allowing the reader to deduce from such events: "Oh, this 'I' who is talking is a stubborn individual, quick to anger and slow to forgive." This can become a plus, for the reader is forced to make inferences and become a participant along with the character as the story unfolds.

One of the most successful uses of the first person narrator is Holden Caulfield in Salinger's *The Catcher in the Rye*. Published in the 1950s, *Catcher* is still read by thousands of young and not so young adults and much of the book's appeal is due to Holden's distinct and individual voice. Once encountered, it can't be forgotten and though often imitated, consciously or unconsciously, it is unique. Read the opening paragraph for yourself and see its effectiveness.

Don't worry about physical description of the "I" narrator, and forget mirrors. Having your "I" look in the mirror and describe herself is too much author manipulation, but your "I" could say that she had spent one whole summer bathing her face in lemon juice, hoping it would bleach out her freckles.

Just as with the limited third person point of view, you may choose to use a first person narrator who is not the central character, but who is one step removed from the problems of the story. *Abby, My Love* (Hadley Irwin) is narrated by Chip, but the book concerns Abby and her relationship to her father. It is graduation night and Abby is on the stage to receive her high school diploma:

> Her head was tilted and the smile still on her lips, but I knew she wasn't really there on stage. Even from where I sat, sweltering, I could see the empty look in her eyes. Once it had puzzled me. It had taken me five years to learn that it meant Abby was gone—absent—not available. She was pulled back so far inside that she was in a different world to which no one ever gained admittance—except me. Once.

The book itself is a flashback of those five years. The author felt that the most effective way of revealing Abby's problem (she was the victim of incest) was through Chip's discovery. Had the story been told from Abby's point of view, explicit details of the abuse would have been difficult to avoid, and if the book were to serve the purpose for which it was written, explicit details were redundant as well as abhorrent. Often, in such cases, less is more.

THE GOOD BEGINNING—HOW TO GO ABOUT IT

The time to flag down your reader's interest is on the first page. Though there are no rules about where a novel should begin, you cannot go far wrong if you start at a point where something is about to happen, where something has already happened, or something is on the verge of happening. To be effective, this "happening" should have an important bearing on the plot that is about to unfold as well as providing an opportunity to introduce at least one or more of the principal characters. Now is the time to give these introductory characters a "handle." Don't worry if the names are not the right ones, for they may change more than once before you are through with your novel.

It is also a good idea, early on, to give your story a definite setting—where the action is to take place, i.e., a city, small town, the country, seaside, the mountains, outer space—and to indicate the time, whether present, recent past, the far-off past or the future. Phrased another way, a good beginning should follow the newspaper formula of the five W's: Who? Where? What? When? Why? As one editor put it, "The first four should be answered early in the game or there will be no game."

True, not all successful novels accomplish these goals in the first chapter, but your novel will have a better chance of getting serious consideration by a publisher if it does. An editor of a major publishing house says he usually needs to read only three pages to determine if a story is worth his while to continue, and he can tell for sure in ten pages. Because certain death is sure to ensue, probably in less than ten pages if your book begins with description or explanation, it is well to keep that fifth "W" in mind. *Why* is this a story worth the telling, and the reading?

Have a Point in Mind

A friend of ours, now the author of more than a dozen successful novels for young adults, discovered two decades ago the importance of having a point in mind. She had spent the day working on a short story she hoped to sell to the *New Yorker,* when her ten-year-old daughter came home from school. The little girl picked up the half-dozen or so pages lying by the typewriter. As she read, not a trace of expression crossed her face. Her mother, who had been hoping for something better than that even from a ten-year-old, called after her as she faded from the room. "Don't you like my story? Don't you think it's good?"

Pausing, the child said delicately, "I liked it, Mom. And I think it's good. I was just wondering when you were going to get to the point."

Our friend laughed. "Later, I read that story over, and it didn't have any point. And it wasn't ever going to have one. I was just going on and on, so into the wastebasket it went."

Although the "point" can be anything you choose, it helps if it is something you feel strongly about. Following are some "points" that generated plots to support full-length, published novels:

> Tragedy within the family (the protagonist's brother contracts AIDS) brings a divided family together
>
> *Night Kites*, by M. E. Kerr

> It is possible to live in isolation (an Indian girl lives alone for years on an island) and still grow as a human being.
>
> *Island of the Blue Dolphins*, by Scott O'Dell

> Jealousy can be conquered. (A young girl deals with her feelings toward a charming and talented twin sister).
>
> *Jacob Have I Loved*, by Katherine Paterson

> The search for identity is difficult but worth pursuing.
>
> *Kim/Kimi*, by Hadley Irwin

> Being sexually accessible does not win a girl the boy she loves.
>
> *Someone To Love Me*, by Jeannette Eyerly

> A fourteen-year-old girl, orphaned and alone, can triumph over adversity.
>
> *Where the Lilies Bloom*, by Vera and Bill Cleaver

Although your novel has a point, this does not mean you are going to moralize. No one, kids least of all, wants to be clobbered over the head with a moral. They get enough lecturing at home. As your main character develops and the plot takes shape, the point will become clear; in fact, readers may not even be aware of what you are up to. They may even think they have made an important discovery all on their own.

One Way to Go

To begin, take any two or three Young Adult novels you admire and in one sentence, no more, write down what each was about. Next, write down, again as briefly as possible, the point the author was making. If it is elusive, look for it until you can pin it down. Now perform the same exercise for the novel you have in mind. With these two goals, on a yellow legal pad, block out ten chapters. The color and size of the legal pad will keep it from getting lost amidst the hundreds of sheets of paper that will flow from your typewriter. Use a separate sheet for each chapter. Do not detach them from the pad. This is going to be a record that will stay with you throughout the writing of your book. You may wind up with more than ten chapters, possibly less, but ten is a good number to aim for.

Now that you have established the point of view from which you will tell your story and have the *point* firmly in mind, give each chapter a heading that expresses that chapter's particular purpose. Patricia Highsmith, widely recognized as one of today's outstanding suspense writers, believes that a starting point for each chapter should begin with the question: How will this chapter advance the story? Discard the chapter if it cannot be made to carry a direction.

A sculptor working in clay first builds an armature to support the figure he intends to model. Only after that does he begin to fill it out, continuing until it assumes the perfection he desires. Your outline is your armature. It is the frame on which you will build your plot and on which you will continue to build until you, too, see your novel come to life.

With the outline of your book on your yellow legal pad before you, jot down under each chapter heading everything you can think of, no matter how trivial, that might fit into that particular chapter. You will probably move some of these bits and pieces around because you will find they fit in better somewhere else. Some of the things that pop into your head you will find no immediate place for. Take another sheet of your legal pad and label it: *Put in Somewhere*. Throughout the writing of your book, you will continue to add to this category, and you will have fun when you can cross another idea out and insert it in the proper place.

Once you have started to write, remember that the outline you have made, even the ending, is not cast in concrete. You may find your character is acting in a different way from the way you intended. A fictional girl who started out to search for the mother who abandoned her when the girl was a baby may have a change of heart and return to the foster parents who raised her.

If some such change in plot happens in your novel, fine. That is what makes writing fun. You will have surprised yourself.

Kenneth Atchity, a teacher of writing at Occidental College, carries this a bit further. He believes that readers want to know in advance and are hoping to be surprised "so they can worry themselves to that point, imagining."

FAMOUS OPENING PASSAGES

Some time back, in what they termed a spirit of summer playfulness, the editors of *The New York Times Book Review* asked a number of authors, "What is your favorite opening passage in a work of literature?" They then recorded the replies under the headline: Famous First Words—Well Begun Is Half Done.

A month later, readers of *The Book Review* jumped into the act with their contributions. In addition to the often-quoted "Call Me Ishmael" from Melville's *Moby Dick,* here are the ones we liked best:

> Happy families are all alike; every unhappy family is unhappy in its own way.
>
> *Anna Karenina* (Tolstoy)

> Mother died today. Or, maybe yesterday. I can't be sure.
>
> *The Stranger* (Camus)

> They threw me off the hayrack about noon.
>
> *The Postman Always Rings Twice* (Cain)

> I am a sick man . . . I am a nasty man . . . a truly unattractive man. I think there is something wrong with my liver.
>
> *Notes From Underground* (Dostoevsky)

In fact, good beginnings are, in themselves, so fascinating a subject that Baird Whitlock collected fifty of them which were then published in book form under the title of *From These Beginnings—Openings of Fifty Major Literary Works.* Of these, Whitlock says the most-quoted beginning paragraph in twentieth-century American prose is from Hemingway's *Farewell to Arms:*

In the late summer of that year we lived in a house in a vil-
lage that looked across the river and the plains to the mountains.
In the bed of the river there were pebbles and boulders, dry and
white in the sun, and the water was clear and swiftly moving and
blue in the channels. Troops went by the house and down the
road and the dust they raised powdered the leaves of the trees. . . .

Whether this satisfies your criteria for the best beginning, or
whether you agree with James Thurber, who reminds us that of
all beginnings "Once upon a time" may still be the best unless
you favor "In the beginning God created Heaven and Earth,"
the fact remains that opening passages must grab readers and
pull them into the story.

This is particularly true in Young Adult novels. Here is a
fine example:

Bobby Zenner disappeared sometime between noon and
one o'clock on the third Saturday of April. Later under police
questioning, Karen would not be able to pinpoint it any more
closely than that. She had been baby-sitting the Zenner children
since ten that morning and Bobby and two of his friends had been
tearing around the house like mad things engaged in one noisy
game after another. Finally, around noon, she had sent them outside to run off energy and to allow her some peace in which to give
lunch to the baby.

It was while she was spooning Jell-O into the mouth of eight-
een-month-old Stephanie that the doorbell rang.

The doorbell, however, does not announce Bobby's arrival
home but Tom Deitz, Karen's boy friend, when the following
conversation takes place:

"Aren't you going to let me in?"
"I can't," said Karen regretfully. "The Zenners . . ."
"Don't want strangers in their house?"
"It's one of the ground rules."
"Am I a stranger?" Tim asked playfully. "Be honest now."
"To them, you are."
He continued to smile at her. "What if I give my solemn
promise not to rip off any of the silverware?"

The outcome is that Karen lets him in and Tim follows her to the kitchen. While she tries to feed the baby, Tim moves up behind her and puts his arms around her waist.

> "Your hair smells good. Like flowers."
> "It's a new shampoo," Karen said inanely. "It's supposed to give extra body."
> "Your body's good enough for me the way it is."

When Tim continues this suggestive talk, accompanying it with attempts at lovemaking, Karen pleads with him saying that it is not as if they were out on a date, and that the Zenners are paying her. Swearing, Tim says he is not trying to rape her and that all he wants is a hello kiss. After some more angry words, he stalks out. Karen is distraught. In addition to the missing Bobby, she has a new worry. Never popular, and still almost unbelieving that she is the dashing senior's girl friend, she thinks she has lost him.

Here in fewer than four pages, Lois Duncan in *The Third Eye* has introduced two principal characters, established time, place, and a mood of suspense. Where is Bobby? Has Karen lost Tim Deitz forever? Do you want to go on reading? Of course, you do, no matter what age you happen to be, and the story gathers momentum as it goes along, for there is a mystery about Karen too, but to tell the entire plot and disclose the meaning of *The Third Eye* would spoil the story.

LOW KEY

Some books begin low key, but the characterizations are so acute and the dialogue so true to life, the situations so similar to their own, that readers are immediately hooked. Such a book is *The Solomon System* by Phyllis Reynolds. It is the story of the Solomon brothers—Ted, sixteen and Nory, thirteen—who survive not only the first estrangement of their lives when their interests begin to diverge, but also the divorce of their parents. Reynolds opens her story like this:

"Ted, tell your father that dinner's ready."

I moved my electronic blob to one corner of the screen where he mushed an invader. I listened for sounds from the den. Sometimes Dad got right up and came. I knew he'd heard.

The electronic blob turned on the guys behind him and mushed them, too.

"Ted!" Mom's voice came again.

I took my feet off the hassock and let the blob have one more go at it before I switched the game off. Still no sound from the den. I got up and slouched across the room.

"He's coming," I said to Mom. I was a blinking messenger service.

We look alike, Dad and I. Both of us are tall, both are skinny—even our noses—and we both have dark hair. Only I'm thirteen and Dad's forty-one, and he's going bald, and I'm not. Nory, my brother, worries about body hair. He'll be sixteen next month, and he hardly has any hair on his legs. He says if he doesn't get hair on his chest he can live with it, but if he doesn't get hair on his legs, he'll kill himself.

"Hey, Nory," I told him once, "some guys don't even have legs, and they manage." [Note the brief flashback]

"Hair's different," Nory said.

Within the next few pages, tension between the boys' mother and father is made clear. The dog, Cleo, has puppies, but who will buy puppies? A grandmother, a fine character, appears but is no help in a deteriorating situation. Later, the boys go off to camp, but the old Solomon system where each always helped out the other isn't working any more. Although everything is still low key, there is no lack of tension and the reader becomes completely wrapped up in the struggle of the Solomon family to work out its problems.

Perhaps the most impressive thing about the following two paragraphs is the compelling, authentic voice of the author writing about what she knows.

Robert Newton Peck's beginning for *A Day No Pigs Would Die* is without frills, but its impact is overwhelming. The book tells the haunting story of a boy's thirteenth year growing up in the Shaker tradition, among the Plain People on a Vermont farm. The first chapter begins simply:

I should have been in school that April day.

But instead I was up on the ridge near the old spar mine above our farm, whipping the gray trunk of a rock maple with a dead stick, and hating Edward Thatcher. During recess, he'd pointed at my clothes and made sport of them. Instead of tying into him, I'd turned tail and run off. And when Miss Malcolm rang the bell to call us back inside, I was halfway home.

Picking up a stone, I threw it into some bracken ferns, hard as I could. Someday that was how hard I was going to light into Edward Thatcher, and make him bleed like a stuck pig. I'd kick him from one end of Vermont to the other, and sorry him good. I'd teach him not to make fun of Shaker ways. He'd never show his face in the town of Learning, ever again. No sir.

In the next fifteen hundred words, Adam comes across a well-to-do neighbor's cow in the process of giving birth. He helps the cow and is terribly mauled, barely escaping with his life.

The character of the narrator Adam is clearly defined, the setting is evident without ostentatious telling, the time is implied, mood firmly established, and most important, something has happened to hint of a plot conflict, and something does happen immediately. These are the five things a good beginning must do. Not only is this entire first chapter an example of almost perfect writing, but the book as a whole illustrates a point we will continue to emphasize—many of the finest books for young people spring from a source deep within their individual authors, a source that is theirs alone. In this case, Peck comes from generations of Yankee farmers, and like Adam of the book, he was raised as a boy in the Shaker way.

Further proof of the value of first hand knowledge is found in *Eyes of Darkness* by Jamake Highwater. A member of the Blackfoot Nation, Highwater has turned to his Indian origins to tell the story of Yesa, brought up in the tradition of the People of the Plains, whose golden youth ends with the coming of the Long Knives, the white men. Sent to a mission school, renamed Alexander East, forced to give up his "savage ways," he is even forbidden to speak the language of his people. The book has additional impact because it is basically true, being a fictional account of the life and works of Dr. Charles Alexander Eastman, once a boy like Yesa, who determines to use his knowledge of medicine to bridge the gap between the white man and the Indian. The book begins like this:

> Alexander East was startled as he sat at his desk staring down at his diploma. It was very late and he could not imagine who could be banging at his door.
> When he opened it he saw Blue Horse and his wife standing uneasily on the step.
> "Much important business, Dr. East. We apologize. We very much apologize for the late hour, but we must talk to you," Blue Horse murmured urgently.
> Scarcely had his guests come inside and been seated, when there was another knock at the door. Captain Sword of the Indian police hurried in, followed by Lieutenant Thunder Deer and almost all the other reservation policemen.
> Alexander was growing anxious to learn the reason for this midnight meeting, but custom required him first to greet each person, hand them some tobacco, and then wait in silence for everyone to smoke in a ceremonial expression of tribal unity.
> After a long silence, Chief Blue Horse finally got up and shook Alexander's hand. Then he began to speak. He explained that he greatly needed the advice of Dr. Alexander East, for a dangerous situation confronted the people of the reservation.

As an exercise, you might see how many of the five criteria of a good beginning you can find in the preceding example.

What young teenager could resist the opening paragraph of Cynthia Voigt's *Izzy, Willy-Nilly*, the triumphant story of sixteen-year-old Isobel, who puts her life together again after an automobile accident that resulted in the loss of one of her legs.

> "Isobel? I'm afraid we're going to have to take it off."
> "Take it off, take it off," I sang, like a vamp song; but I don't think I actually did, and I know my laughter stayed locked inside my head. I think my voice did too.
> "Isobel. Can you hear me?"
> I didn't know. I didn't think so.
> *It* was my leg. I went to sleep.

In *Rear-View Mirrors,* Paul Fleischman draws readers in by a first paragraph that supplies the near-perfect voice of the narrator, an introduction to the principal characters, a sense of time and place, and a strong hint of the plot that is about to unfold.

> I grew up acquainted with my father neither by sight nor by scent, but solely by report. He was like a distant land known only through travelers' tales, an inhospitable realm where strange and shocking customs survived. There, moths and butterflies were stalked, caught, dried, labeled, and displayed on the walls of every room, as if they were charms against evil spirits. Pea soup and bagels were the staple foods. The Boston Red Sox were noisily worshipped there and the tobacco left ritually burned, its foul-smelling smoke unknown in our house, constantly rising upward like incense. My mother had been there, carrying me out of that country when I was eight months old. As my father, in the sixteen years after, hadn't found time to once call or write, I grew up to be grateful she'd taken me with her. She was his ex-wife; I was his ex-daughter.

Looking back over these beginnings, it is easy to see not only how varied they are but how appropriate each is to the story about to be told. You will also notice that *The Solomon System, The Day No Pigs Would Die, Izzy, Willy-Nilly* and *Rear-View Mirrors* are "I" stories and each has a voice suitable to each individual story. Here, we are not referring to voice as tonal quality nor in its grammatical sense of active and passive but to the voices with which the "I" narrators express themselves.

If you are planning to write an "I" story, remember that the voice must be accurate in every detail and that from the first sentence it must bespeak of the narrator: sex, race, background, education, temperament, even the part of the country or the era in which the narrator lives.

SUMMING UP

• Establish the point of view from which your story is going to be told.

- Chart your course with an outline.
- Be aware of the five criteria for a good beginning.
- Keep your story moving. There is a difference between effective detail and narrative clutter.
- Answer, the best you can, the who, what, where, and when of good first chapters.
- Always keep that fifth "W" in mind. It contains the *point* of your story. If you don't know *why* you are writing this book, it is doubtful that your readers will know or care either.

WHAT A CHARACTER!

———◆———

A fixture in practically every major city in the country before television was the stock company. Throughout the winter season, a group of resident actors with a downtown theater as a base performed a series of popular plays. These were either something that in that day were called drawing room comedies, or they were mystery dramas. While one play was running, another was in rehearsal.

In each play there was always the leading man, handsome and debonair, and, to match, a lovely leading lady. Always there were the ingenue, young and beautiful, and of course a villain or, if not a villain, another less desirable suitor for the hand of the ingenue, or a character planning to come between a husband and wife and break up the marriage. And what kind of play would you have without a crusty but lovable old father and a society-type mother? Often there was a monocled British lord; a butler, too, was a necessity, as was a parlor maid and policeman, Irish, naturally.

Although there was a good deal of switching around of the juicier or more important roles, *the roles themselves* did not change. The leading man was always handsome and debonair, the leading lady, suave and beautiful; the ingenue, young and delightful; the old father, always crusty; the society-type mother, always silly; the villain, villainous; the butler, supercilious. In fact, stock theater roles became as one-dimensional as paper dolls; their emotions, their actions and reactions correspondingly thin and always predictable.

Though the stock company—not to be confused with the prestigious repertory companies in many major cities—is no more, stock characters are still around. Known as "stereotypes," they regularly make their appearance in romance-type paperbacks and westerns. There is nothing wrong with them if this is your intent. If, however, you are aiming your novel at the hardcover Young Adult market with hefty sales to libraries and the possibility of quality paperback publication later on, bear in mind that believable characters take care and planning.

Though young teens will become wiser as they grow older and see more than the surface beauty or attractiveness of their peers, looks are important to them and often are the key to popularity which, of course, though often publicly disdained, is secretly admired and coveted. Therefore, readers want to know how the principal characters *look*. This involves, first, their age.

Because it depends in large part on the age of the reader for whom you are writing, age should be selected carefully. Though twelve or thirteen-year-olds will read books about those younger than themselves, by most these are considered "baby books." The preference of most girls of this age is for books whose characters are fifteen or sixteen or even older, who go out with boys and have one foot in the grown-up world to which they aspire. Subteen and young teen boys, likewise, prefer to read books about boys older than they are, who are winning important games or triumphing over difficulties on land, sea, or air— or outer space. Slightly older teens, both boys and girls, enjoy books about young people who are in college or working.

Readers are also interested in the approximate shape and size, hair and eye color, as well as any redeeming or unredeeming features of the principal characters. Such details should not be listed in police-blotter type descriptions and certainly not at the beginning of the book, but be worked in to become a part of the whole.

Despite the fact that teens have much in common—they do tend to embrace the same fads in clothing, listen to the same kind of music, talk the same language—the term *typical teenager* is a misnomer and it is best to erase it both from your mind and your written vocabulary. Teens are as varied as their fingerprints. Think of *individuals*, not just the ones you are going to write about, but the ones who will some day be reading your book.

READER RECOGNITION

When a teenage reader says, "That's *me* in that book!" or "Whoever wrote that book must know my dad," or "I know a kid just like that," you, as an author, have succeeded in establishing reader recognition, not just a plus for a book but a *must*. For this to be achieved, characters must be given personalities suitable to the part they are to play. Whether they are timid, outgoing, secretive, brazen, cowardly, courageous, tenacious, or conniving, they must have particular mannerisms, individual ways of talking, walking, or acting. Some will have irritating habits. Are they always interrupting? Twisting a lock of hair? Flirting? Doodling? Are they usually late for whatever is going on?

What they must *not* be is too perfect—nor too bad. The character on whom the author lavishes too many perfections becomes unbelievable, a caricature. Likewise, the character who is too bad loses credibility. In real life, people, including teenagers, are seldom all good or all bad. Book people should be the same. Certain flaws, in fact, tend to make a character more real and appealing. Overcoming the flaw, one that teenagers themselves may possess, can become a conflict that propels the plot. Even serious weaknesses such as addiction to drugs or alcohol that possibly, in the course of your story, result in the death or injury of another person, can be forgiven by young adult readers if the character is sorry, does penance, and makes amends.

Flaws and serious weaknesses, however, are one thing. Character *defects*, or something deep within that person, is another. If the character is to win the sympathy of the reader (as a *main* character or protagonist must), cruelty in any form, whether to a person or animal, should be avoided. Equally unsympathetic is the character who indulges in wanton destruction, major vandalism, muggings, or the inflicting of intentional injury on an innocent person.

Adult Characters

Parents, teachers, older brothers and sisters, neighbors, employers, all play a large part in the life of young people. When these adult figures appear in books, they must be as real and recognizable as your teenage characters with whom they come in contact. A decision you will have to make sometime during the planning of your story is how important in developing the theme of your story these people are. Often, if the protagonist's parents are not to be a determining factor in the conflict of the story, authors will have them hovering offstage as stock or flat characters. This is perfectly permissible and even advisable, since the length of an average teenage novel does not permit space for the full development of a large cast of characters.

In motion pictures there are extras or walk-on parts necessary to create reality. In a novel these extras might appear as a school crossing guard, a janitor, a salesperson in a department store. Such adult characters need not be developed. Whether the character is a member of the protagonist's family or someone encountered by chance, the amount of development required depends upon the extent to which that character contributes to the resolution of the novel's central conflict. In Zindel's *The Pigman*, the story revolves around an adult character who must come alive to the reader. The same is true of Mrs. Frankweiler in *From the Mixed-up Files of Mrs. Basil E. Frankweiler* by Konigsburg. The development of her character is necessary for the plot to evolve. Both Mr. Pigman and Mrs. Frankweiler are real people on the page. On the other hand, the "chieftain of the white men," the captain of the Aleut ship that comes to remove the inhabitants of the island in O'Dell's *Island of the Blue Dolphins*, is a stock character fulfilling a necessary function but otherwise of no particular interest.

Name of the Game

Whether the part the character plays is large or small, the name must fit the part, and the part must be carefully delineated. Jack Smith, columnist for *The Los Angeles Times*, raises an interesting question in that connection. After commenting that "Call me

Ishmael" is probably the most famous first line in American literature, he writes, "I think it was sly of Melville to call his narrator Ishmael. What if his name had been Clarence? Or Fred? Would 'Call me Clarence' have been a good enough beginning? 'Call me Fred?' "

Just as with so many other words, names carry all sorts of connotations, the various associations or suggested significance a name can evoke. Names like Judas or Hitler used in a contemporary book would certainly cause a negative reaction on the part of the reader. On a more subtle level, think of your own varied reactions to these names: Penny, Clara, Mable, Cindy, Elmer, Jon, Homer. For whatever reason, you would probably associate each name with a different era, a different physical characteristic, perhaps even a different geographic location. It is not a matter of logic. It is a matter of subjective response. Sometimes a carefully chosen name, one that seems right in the beginning, turns out to be a stumbling block for a writer. If a name bothers you, change it.

Before you name your principal character or any character in your book who plays more than a minor part, you must know how your characters look, how they feel, the kind of clothes they wear, what their economic position is. Not until she was writing the last page of *Someone To Love Me* (Eyerly) did the author know that the name of Patrice's illegitimate baby boy, who for almost a year had been nameless, was *Chance*. Sometimes a name can be so elusive as to cause despair. What to do? Some authors run through the alphabet, coming up with every name they can think of from A to Z. Perhaps Max Beerbohm did this when he wrote *Zuleika Dobson*.

One writer of our acquaintance bought a book called *What to Name the Baby* at her local supermarket. Others turn to the telephone directory, using different first and last names to form new combinations. Names can also be made up out of whole cloth. Even the keyboard of your typewriter can provide inspiration. *Shift* might be a good surname. *Shiftlock* sounds too much like *The Merchant of Venice*. Of course, it could be spelled *Schift* if the person had a Germanic background. Hermann Schift, perhaps.

Names of birds also come in handy. We know of a fictional

school principal who is named Mr. Merganser. And how about Robin or Lark for a girl's first name? For last names, Starling, Warbler, Coot, Grosbeak, Sparrow, and Redstart all have possiblities as do dozens more.

And how do you suppose L. Frank Baum ever came up with the name of "Oz" for the marvelous never-never land he created for Dorothy, Scarecrow, Tin Woodman, and the Cowardly Lion? He told how in an interview printed in the May 10, 1903, issue of *The St. Louis Republic:*

> I have a little cabinet letter file on my desk in front of me. I was thinking and wondering about a title for my story and I had settled on "Wizard" as part of it. My gaze was caught by the gilt letters on the three drawers of the cabinet. The first was A-G; the next drawer was labeled H-N and on the last were the letters O-Z.

It took more than three tries with the title of the book—one was *From Kansas to Fairyland*—before he thought of the one that pleased the editors of the publishing house: *The Wonderful Wizard of Oz.*

A practice not nearly so in vogue as it was in the nineteenth century but which can still be effective if slyly done is "name playing." After more than a hundred years, readers are laughing at the doctor in *Barchester Towers* whose name is Dr. Fullgrave and that of the country parson with twelve children who is called the Reverend Quiverfull.

Always with names it is best to be cautious. Readers frequently see themselves in a book, and if the portrait is an unflattering one, sometimes take the poor author to court in a defamation of character suit. Those disclaimers in the front of novels that "The characters in this book are fictitious and bear no resemblance to any persons living or dead" have a sound reason for being there. Occasions can still arrive when that is not enough.

A common mistake, and one frequently made, but fortunately correctable, is giving two of the important characters names that begin with the same letter. As fine a writer as Paul Scott did so in *The Raj Quartet,* a four-volume work that won acclaim as a Masterpiece Theater series. He named two widely disparate individuals, one a mother-in-law, the other a daughter-in-law, Mable and Mildred Layton. The letter "M" did it. At least half of the time, the reader had to stop momentarily to sort out who was speaking or being spoken to.

Although you can work on naming your characters before you ever sit down to start your novel, when the day finally comes that it can be put off no longer or—horrors!—you have already started and are already stuck on page three—this is a good way to begin: Take a fresh sheet of paper. A yellow, lined legal pad is good for this purpose. At the top, write CAST OF CHARACTERS just as it would appear on the program of a Broadway play or one given by your local little theater group.

1. Opposite each name, allowing several lines for each character, write in an identifying description. These need be only a few words, though it is a good idea to include the person's primary characteristic. You probably know your principal characters so well you need no reminder about the way they look.
2. Because your principal characters most likely have a family, group these names together: Mother, Father, Brothers, Sisters, Uncles, Aunts, Cousins or Guardian, whoever.
3. Next comes best friend. It helps if your character has someone to talk to. Beware of too much interior thinking and remembering: they slow the story down.
4. If your novel takes place during the school year, add some classmates. If it takes place in the summer, improvise.
5. Add some teachers—maybe one who is on the side of your protagonist, and another who plays the part of the bad guy, someone always useful to have around.
6. Sometimes a pet comes in handy. Horses are always good characters. Dogs can be particularly useful. It has been said that a person could write a best selling novel if he would call it *Abraham Lincoln's Doctor's Dog.*

Some of the initial cast of characters will prove superfluous as you write. If they don't serve a purpose, get them out of there. One young novelist had so many characters that by the end of her story she had to have most of them jump over a cliff and perish.

Here's the way the cast of characters for *He's My Baby, Now* (Eyerly) looked before the actual writing began:

Charles Elderbury—the boy
Pamela Elderbury—his mother
Daisy—mother of the baby
Baby—Just "Baby"
Charlotte Penrose—Charles' grandmother (she's not like most)
Mr. Farley—Manager of supermarket where Charles works
Jeff—Charles' best friend

Other characters were added as needed and named as they came on stage. These included Lucy Twining, a new girl friend for Charles; Mr. Bascomb, a beau for Charles' mother, Macho Muriel, fastest check-out person at the supermarket, who is roughly the same size and shape as the six-foot refrigerator standing in Charles' kitchen at home; Hubert Turnquist, also a new father, who is a fellow-employee at Farley's; plus a few walk-on parts.

The simple act of putting your Cast of Characters on paper will be the first step in turning them into real people. After that, who knows what will happen?

BUILDING CHARACTER

Anyone creating not just a character but a real person frequently lays a solid foundation for future books. This is what Lois Lowry did with her first Anastasia book, a character for which she is probably best known. Though later books do not comprise a series in any sense of the word, in each of them Anastasia, the bright daughter of a college professor/poet/painter, learns the various lessons of life from the disruption of moving to the death of a grandmother. In another book, Anastasia experiences the humiliation of being the only girl in the seventh grade who can't climb the ropes in gym class. Though this doesn't sound like the greatest theme in the world, the character of Anastasia makes it a charming and interesting book.

For the Young Adult novel, no one does characterization better than S. E. Hinton. In the first sentence of *That Was Then, This Is Now*, the story of two boys, best friends from childhood, who grow apart when Byron finds that Mark is pushing drugs to young kids, we not only have a good first sentence, but our first clue as to the kind of kids they are: "Mark and me went down to the bar/pool hall about two or three blocks from where we lived with the sole purpose of making some money."

We *see* the boys only a few pages later when Byron says of himself, "I'm a big guy, dark hair and eyes—the kind who looks like a Saint Bernard puppy, which I don't mind as most chicks cannot resist a Saint Bernard puppy. Mark was small and compact with strange golden eyes and hair to match and a grin like a friendly lion." Their friend, M&M, becomes as real to readers as if his photograph were before their eyes, with these few short sentences:

> He always had this wide-eyed, intent trusting look on his face, but sometimes he smiled and when he did it was really great. He was an awful nice kid even if he was a little strange.
>
> He had big gray eyes—the kind you see on war orphan posters—and charcoal colored hair down past his ears and down to his eyebrows. He probably would have grown a beard except thirteen was too young for it. He always wore an old army jacket that was too big for him and went barefoot even when it started getting cold.

In Judy Blume's *Tiger Eyes*, Lenaya, Tiger's best friend, who appears only briefly, is memorably characterized thus: "Lenaya is six feet one, skinny and black. Everyone assumes she must be great at basketball, but the truth is, she hates the game. She'd rather do an experiment with her chemistry set or read a book on genetics." Because of Lenaya's differentness, no one will confuse her with another girl who later becomes Tiger's best friend.

M. E. Kerr, in *Night Kites*, pictures two very different girl characters like this, both seen through the eyes of the central boy character:

> I loved Dill's looks. She had a style that was both sweet and tough. She was pretty, but she was also boyish. She had this great face; strong white teeth, always a tan left over from summer, straight black hair she liked to wear very short, slicked back almost like a boy's cut. That day she had on the gold hoop earrings I'd given her for her birthday. She didn't have Nicki's full figure—she had practically no breasts. She had a great way of talking

out of one side of her mouth, as though what she was saying had to be sneaked into any conversation. But Dill wasn't really shy. I was her first real boyfriend.

And here's Nicki:

> I don't think I'd ever seen Nicki in pants, not even when she was on the back of Ski's motorcycle. She just never wore them. Dill was in a skirt that day, too, the pom-pon outfit, with the very short maroon skirt and the white sweater.
>
> But Dill usually wore Guess? jeans or cords. Nicki wore outfits, costumes; that day some kind of navy blue knee-length sweat shirt with Day-Glo socks and dark gladiator sandals. You didn't expect such a thin girl to fill out a baggy sweat shirt the way Nicki did. You expected the long, thin legs, and she had long blond hair, the soft, shiny kind that fell over one eye.
>
> Nicki was always brushing it back to look at you with those light-green eyes, as though she was sizing you up, as though she was telling you she could handle you no matter who you were.

A character in a fine adult novel, Gail Godwin's *Finishing School,* makes an appearance that is about as brief as it is possible to make, but we not only *see* her "as a young, neat, sexless person with straight teeth," but we know a good deal more about her when the narrator says, "She smiled, showing her white teeth, and then recrossed her legs chastely behind her word processor. I was sure she was the kind of girl who wore white cotton panties under her pantyhose."

Elsewhere we insist on the rule, "Show. Don't tell." It holds equally true when you are building a character. The emphasis here is on the word *building,* as compared to the example above which is a one-time vignette.

If Janie is five feet tall, has red hair and green eyes and is hot-tempered, you are not going to throw all this information at your reader at one time and in so many words. It can come out in natural stages and part of the dialogue like this:

> "Don't call me Shrimp," Janie said.
> Though she was smiling, Deever wasn't fooled. Her eyes had turned a certain electric shade of green. Even her curly, copper-colored hair that reminded him of one of those scouring pads

his mother kept in the kitchen seemed to send off sparks.

"Sorry, Shrimp," he said, ducking as he said it. "I was only going to ask you to the . . ."

He didn't finish. Janie had already turned and was off down the hall.

There, you have provided the groundwork. Janie is a small girl with copper-colored hair which sounds much more attractive than saying it is red, eyes that are a certain electric shade of green, and what is more, she has a hot temper.

Such descriptive details can be used time and time again, in one way or another. For example, Janie's hair can "glow in the darkness" or "Janie had washed her hair and as she rubbed it dry, every strand stood as erect as if it had been wired for sound." About Janie's size: "Standing there, Janie seemed to grow until she was almost as tall as Marcia." Or "Janie insisted she had grown, but she had not. Stretch as she might she missed five feet by a quarter of an inch." Janie's temper, which we know is hot: "Janie boiled over when she heard the news." How about, "Janie was so angry even her skin was hot to the touch."

If Tom is awkward, don't *say* Tom is awkward. *Show* him being awkward.

Jason hadn't seen Tom since school was out in May. In the meantime, it looked as if he had grown another couple of inches and was having trouble with his hands and feet. Before the period ended he had knocked over a vase of flowers on Miss Pritchard's desk, spilling water all over everything. Jason smiled.

Here is an unlooked-for bonus in this short paragraph. It is the sentence, "Jason smiled." Because Jason is amused by Tom's awkwardness and his attitude is condescending, we do not like him. This gives you two blocks to build on: Tom's awkwardness and Jason's superciliousness.

Crime and Punishment

If you are having trouble developing a character, it may be time to remember William S. Gilbert's lines from the opera *The Mika-*

do. "My object all sublime," sings the Mikado, "I shall achieve in time—to let the punishment fit the crime."

To rephrase for our purposes: Let the character fit the conflict (call it the "point," if you wish) that is at the heart of your novel. Show not only *how* the protagonist reacts to a given situation—say, to the death of a parent—but the *why.* If unmoved, or seemingly so, how does the protagonist act? And why? What is said or done? *There must be motivation for all speech and action.* Look for it and build your character accordingly.

Another route to go in developing character is to think *characteristic* rather than *character.* You can begin with people you know, those within your family, at work, school, or in any social situation, applying one outstanding characteristic to each. It is a fair guess that the character of Mr. Harding, who plays an imaginary cello in times of stress throughout the more than five hundred pages of *The Warden* and *Barchester Towers,* two of Anthony Trollope's best-loved novels, was inspired by someone whom the author knew. Because the trait described was so endearing, Mr. Harding gained a few million more admirers when he became visible, still playing his imaginary cello, on TV's Masterpiece Theater production of Trollope's books, published more than one hundred and forty years ago.

It is well to remember, however, that in following this example you use *only* the characteristic, *not* the person. Using an actual person can cause you trouble because it can limit you in developing a character who might be far more interesting than the person from whom you got your inspiration. Inserting a personal friend into your story can hamper characterization because, paradoxically, you may know too much about your friend.

When you attempt to guide her through the intricacies of the plot, you will find the real person dominating your fictional character. Your characterization, thus, becomes photographic rather than artistic. But this does not preclude taking one dominant characteristic from a real person and building a fictional character on that one trait. Take Trollope's Mr. Harding as a model. Once you have settled on a primary characteristic, make the most of it.

It is from Trollope, too, that we learn another secret of characterization. Just as people in real life change and become better or worse as temptation or conscience guides them, so must characters in your book. He even recommends that you make note of such changes and on the last day of each month recorded make sure that every person in your novel is a month older than when you began.

Following Trollope's rule to its logical conclusion, by the time a book ends the principal character should be different from what he was when you began. If your main character has not become a better person or, conversely, a worse person, succeeded or failed in a matter of great importance, discovered an unknown skill or learned that there are different ways of winning, it might be best to do some rethinking of your basic idea.

SUMMING UP

Toddlers often make up an imaginary friend who becomes very real to them. Skip back in time and let your main character become your imaginary friend. Talk to her. Share your life and thoughts with her. Let her inhabit your home. Become so well acquainted with this imaginary character that she becomes one of the family.

Then when you begin to reveal this friend to your readers, choose carefully the methods you will use.

1. Description in the words of another character. *"Sorry, Shrimp,"* *he said.* The reader knows Janie is short in stature.
2. Author explanation. Use sparingly. Show more often than tell.
3. Change. Allow your character to grow day by day, week by week, page by page.
4. Dialogue. Let your characters reveal themselves through conversation.
5. Thoughts or stream-of-consciousness.
6. Details of setting to reinforce individual traits. Who could think of Huck Finn without the Mississippi River?
7. Mannerisms.
8. Recurring object or image closely associated with a character. Mr. Harding's cello.
9. Appropriate name.
10. Action.

seven

HOW LONG IS HIS HAIR? HOW SHORT IS HER SKIRT?

—————◆—————

If you are writing a historical novel, dress, customs, habits of speech will be part of the past era. If you choose to write a teen-age romance, the shelf life of your book may be so short that the reader will find nothing outdated. But if you are writing a story that you hope will stay in print through a third edition (or for-ever), styles, language, and attitudes are of some concern.

Perhaps, as a beginning writer, you have decided on a con-temporary novel—in the 1980s. You know the geographical set-ting you choose will be dictated, in part, by the possibilities it of-fers the story and in part by what you know well. However, as with every other aspect of writing, a danger lurks. You may be more accustomed to local habits and idiosyncrasies than your potential editor or reader, and too many regionalisms may creep into your story.

In *Bring to a Boil and Separate* (Hadley Irwin) the about-to-be-divorced veterinarian father of the central character walks toward her through the crowd at a horse show. She spots him im-mediately because of his height and because of the *seed-corn cap* he is wearing. Now, in the Midwest, where the story takes place, that is a perfectly simple and accurate description of an item of apparel. The father is wearing a billed, ventilated cap with the name of some seed corn company emblazoned on the front. It was not obvious to the Eastern editor until a cap was sent to her with directions for washing: throw it in a washing machine and stretch it over a three-pound coffee can for drying. Her reply, as a single parent, was "What's a three-pound coffee can?" The cap disappeared from the story.

In *Moon and Me* (Hadley Irwin), Moon sends a postcard to AJ, who is in Minnesota. He tells her that he needs to earn money, so he has taken a job *walking beans*. This began a series of letters between the author and the editor in New York. "Are you being funny? Why would anyone walk on beans? Are you being deliberately obscure?"

Rather than having to explain that the term means walking through a forty-acre field of soy beans and pulling or cutting the weeds between the rows, the authors decided on the easy way out. "Just say he is detasseling corn."

The next letter was a short one: "Why would anyone in his right mind go through a garden pulling the top of corn stalks? Couldn't Moon be out picking tomatoes?"

Again, instead of an explanation of the history of seed corn fields in Iowa as well as cross-pollination, or instead of pointing out that the only tomatoes grown are in backyard gardens, the authors suggested that Moon might be helping bale hay. This worked. There seem to be horses almost everywhere, and they eat hay which comes in bales.

Just as regionalism has its hazards, so does description of dress, fads, and slang. The preppy look, the Valley look, the punk look that were part of the early eighties will probably soon be archaic. "Why is her hair dyed green and orange? Why does he have a safety pin in his ear lobe?" Even length of hair can be a problem. Hair styles change as quickly as hem lengths.

In *Goodbye to Budapest* (Eyerly) the author avoided the hair problem by describing Andras, the hero, as "wearing the same brown raincoat he'd worn in London, the cinched-in belt too long because of the narrowness of his waist, the same black curling hair that was, in length, just right." This allowed the reader to imagine Andras' hair any length, even if it were down to his waist.

Fads present still another danger. Remember the hula

hoop, pet rocks, Frisbees? Even ghetto-blasters and Walkmans may have disappeared soon after you get the words on the page. That is equally true of slang. One day's "peachy-keen" can become another day's "fantastic" before you can reach for your Funk and Wagnall's. Of course, if you are writing a book of nostalgia, you deliberately attempt to date the novel. Again, the writer's purpose will dictate the choices in these matters.

ANACHRONISMS

A chronological error in placing some one or something in the wrong time frame is considered an anachronism. Even Shakespeare was guilty in *Julius Caesar,* when he had Caesar ask, "What is't o'clock?" and Brutus dutifully answers, "Caesar, 'tis strucken eight." Clocks were not invented in 44 BC. Perhaps this error was not of Shakespeare's doing, but of a scrivener who copied his various folios, but anachronisms are sure to be spotted by eagle-eyed critics.

In *I Be Somebody* (Hadley Irwin), set in 1910 in Oklahoma, it was necessary for the authors to research carefully the make and description of a car that appeared in one scene. Likewise it was necessary to research trains of 1910 as well as dress, food, flora, fauna, farm implements, fishing gear, one-room schoolhouses, and language.

So time lays traps for the unwary writer in terms of language, style, even the small bits of everyday life that we take for granted. The same holds true for what might be called popular morality—that is, prevalent attitudes toward sexual behavior.

WHAT ABOUT SEX

Sex, like food, is more fun to share than to read about; but write about it, in one of its infinite variations, you probably will. And chances are that someone, somewhere, will object to what you have written. The same could be said of writing about drugs, violence, religion, or politics. Take heart.

In many ways, the matter of sexuality or sexual behavior occupies less space in a novel than most potential censors would admit. Even if the book centers on some form of sexual behavior, other things claim the reader's attention; other events and concerns are part of the characters' lives. With few exceptions, characters do not spend all their time thinking about or participating in sexual activity.

From the once earth-shaking question of whether or not a character should kiss on the first date, Young Adult literature has moved on to more difficult subjects: teenage pregnancy, masturbation, homosexuality, rape, incest. That these subjects are not treated lightly or dishonestly is evident because the characters who confront or are involved with these situations are NOT stereotypic; they are real human beings of varying ethnic, economic, and educational backgrounds. They are people with whom the reader can identify; they are people who, without pointing a moral, do suggest or explore possible solutions to the problems.

KEEP YOUR READER IN MIND

Although a boy or girl is legally considered a child until age eighteen, your reader will not be interested in what used to be called "kiddie books." By the time your readers are in junior high, they will have acquired more sexual awareness, a larger vocabulary of gutter words, and pseudoexperiences from television viewing than did their parents at the same age. Yet, the sad fact is, that despite this "knowledge," most are woefully ignorant. Currently, with over a million teenagers becoming pregnant and either bearing their babies or having abortions, how can one think otherwise? A sex counselor for the public schools in a large midwestern city kept track of the questions asked him in several separate sessions with groups of junior high boys and girls. Some sample questions from the boys include "What's the world's biggest prick measurement?" "Is something wrong if you have one testicle lower than the other?" "When and where can you masturbate safely?" "What's a female cock called?" "How tough is that hymen thing?" "What's the soonest a boy should screw a girl?" "How do you know you won't give your kid too many chromosomes?" "How much blood does a girl lose during her period?" "Can squeezing a girl's breasts give her cancer?" "What's wrong with using Saran Wrap or Cokes as contraceptives?"

Sample questions from the girls were no less interesting: "What's the clitoris for?" "Where, actually, is it?" "Will masturbation make my vagina bigger?" "Can sexual intercourse get to be habit-forming?" "Does a guy ever have a safe period?" "Do girls ever turn queer?" "Is mono a form of VD?" "Can a girl have a baby by her father?" "How does a girl stop a boy when she doesn't want to go any further?" "How big does the penis get when it is big?"

Children like these, if not facing the problem of sex with colossal ignorance, are up against other problems just as tough and difficult to deal with as any they will face when they are grown. Young Adult novels can, and frequently do, provide a way out of this wasteland. Though they may not provide a solution, they can give a means of coping with life.

HOW FAR IS TOO FAR?

Virtually no subject is taboo in Young Adult literature. As one librarian stated, "If a book is tastefully done and addresses the issue, I would not hesitate to include it in my library."

The choice of subject matter for the book you write is yours to make. If you are not comfortable reading teenage books because of implicit or explicit sexual scenes or because of language that is distasteful to you, that is not the kind of book for you to write. Librarians dealing with young people often say such books are often read only for the spicy parts. One does not have to be a Sherlock Holmes to determine which pages have been ruffled with use and those which have remained unread.

It should be noted, however, that times change. In recent years the entire country has become more conservative, and attempts to ban various Young Adult books from public libraries have become more frequent. Naturally editors and publishers who are well into market research tend to be conservative, too, and partial to the "safe" novel—novels which can ride out the storms of censorship. However, if Young Adult literature is to "hold a mirror up to life," authors must be willing to write on risky subjects and dare to bring about change. Knowledge does not corrupt.

If you as a writer have something to say, have faith in what you say, and say it well, you'll find a publisher. Pacesetting is risky business, but there is no need for a fresh, innovative writer to follow the crowd. If you have a bent for history or you have an imagination lively enough to people a novel with space creatures, or you have an understanding of today's young people caught up in a world they did not make, or if you simply have the ability to look into the hearts of a boy and girl in love, you need only concern yourself with one thing: be sure you have a story to tell.

The novel, *I'll Get There, It Better Be Worth the Trip* by John Donovan (1970), in which a homosexual episode in the lives of two thirteen-year-old boys forms a major part of the story, caused Ursula Nordstrom, a highly respected editor of children's books, to say, "The walls crumble down, just a little, all the time."

As young adults insist on truth and quality in their selection of books to read, authors and publishers oblige with such titles as *He's My Baby, Now* (Eyerly) concerning a young boy facing the problem of fathering an illegitimate child, *Sticks and Stones* (Hall) of the confusion of a young boy who has been labeled homosexual by a small community, *Abby, My Love* (Hadley Irwin) of a young man's discovery that his Abby is a victim of incest, or *Forever* (Blume) where teenagers face their first sexual experience.

CURSES

Bad language, however, is something else again. It is not a necessary adjunct. A book on any subject can be written without the use of any four-letter words or other vulgarities.

Just as beauty is said to be in the eye of the beholder, so is bad language in the eye of the reader. A word that some young persons might sail over without even a backward glance may send the child next door scuttling to a parent in a state of shock.

In the latter instance, possibly within twenty-four hours, the irate parent will request the book be removed from the shelves of all the schools' libraries. Should the book have come from the Public Library, the request that the book be banned will be made to the library's board of directors.

Such a furor usually winds up on the front page of the newspaper. School board members read and huddle, reconsideration committees meet, the Public Library announces itself as standing firm, all of which results in increased attention and sale of the book.

Another scenario comes from the other direction. This time, a librarian reads a book with the idea in mind of purchasing it for the library. She is turned off by the book and does *not* buy it. "Money is too scarce," she says, firmly, "for a book like *that*."

One well-known author of Young Adult books, who doesn't consider herself a "dirty writer" in any sense of the word, has had several of her many novels removed from the shelves of public libraries in small midwestern cities.

So-called bad language is a topic that at intervals rears its head in the letters column of *The American Library,* the official magazine of the prestigious and influential American Library Association. In response to letters, in two previous issues, from librarians complaining about bad language in Young Adult novels, a third librarian in the Chicago area wrote in reply:

> Authors who use swear words in young adult literature are reflecting a normal progression of growth found in virtually all young people. Most try these words in one way or another as they get older. Many drop them completely as they get older still. Others absorb them into their regular vocabulary.
>
> Either way, these are words only, a form of expression. Used to excess they're ridiculous; used as they are in YA lit they're usual and acceptable.
>
> It's hard enough for YA's to read. Giving them sanitized versions of books won't make things any better. These kids are facing much more than we did, at an earlier age. A few swear words in a book won't hurt them.

With these pros and cons in mind, the choice to use or not to use, is yours. Questionable words, of course, can be deleted from a manuscript, though there is a strong possibility the sentence will have to be rewritten. After all, at the last moment you can't very well substitute "Oh! Shucks!" for its more common and contemporary equivalent when the car slips off the jack while Davie is changing the tire. It might be better simply to say, in the first place, "Davie swore."

The question still remains, however, about what to do with an explicit sexual scene. To paraphrase the 1950s, how far is all the way? The answer gets back to a couple of basics: what happens in the world of the novel should depend on the characters themselves, and the point of view determines how much the reader actually shares. Perhaps the final question is: Are you writing a novel or a sex manual? Ultimately the solution is in the mind of the author as to what is aesthetically, logically, or personally pleasing.

The authors of *Abby, My Love,* which deals with incest, had talked about the book for at least four years before they began the first draft. They knew the subject was important, they knew it had to be written as honestly as they could, but they did not want to write explicit sexual scenes between the father and daughter. Here a chance remark by a school librarian offered the solution. "It's a book that should be written," the librarian said, "It would be important for the victim, of course, but just as important for the best friend. There always is one, you know—the best friend who senses something is wrong, but does not understand."

That comment made clear that the point of view could be that of a friend, not the victim herself, and that reader and friend could slowly discover, without sensationalism, the secret pain of Abby's life. Perhaps the Greek playwrights were accurate—let the shocking occur off stage. Must we watch Oedipus put out his eyes?

TO TELL THE TRUTH

The world presented in young adult literature must be a real world or else you as an author are lying. There are in the world today threats of nuclear holocaust, the raping of our natural resources, an inequality among races and numerous social problems such as hunger, suicide, alcoholism, drug abuse, violence, war, murder. Write about real human beings in their infinite variety of ethnicity, age, experience, ugliness, and beauty.

In creating fictional reality on the page, you must be true to the customs, attitudes, and mores of the society about which you are writing as well as the language used to express those abstractions. As an author, you are responsible *to* your story and *to* your audience, which means that you must make value judgments about the situations you present as well as the language in which it is couched. Be true to yourself and you will not be false to your reader.

◆ e i g h t ◆

HE SAID, SHE SAID

◆———◆———◆

If fiction is artful lying, dialogue is pure deception. In either case only an approximation of reality, not reality itself, appears on the page. Tape a casual, spontaneous conversation and transcribe it to paper. What was exciting and alive to the ear is now erratic, unintelligible, and dull. Most of all, it appears unrealistic. Good dialogue is not actual speech, but it contains the flavor of actual speech.

So why write dialogue at all when it could be so easy to avoid by letting the author tell the story? Because strong, active narrative demands *showing,* not *telling,* and one of the best means of achieving *showing* is through dialogue, between or among characters or within one character's mind—interior monologue. The purpose of dialogue is always to help create character, reveal relationships, and advance the plot. Conversation for its own sake is a terrible waste of quotation marks as well as dull reading.

The uses and effects of dialogue are many. Irony can spring from the differences between what characters say and what they think. Those sometimes awkward bits of exposition, background, history, past events can be reduced from paragraphs of author explanation to a short conversation between two characters. But make sure the characters are not just mouthpieces for the author but *really are* exchanging bits of informa-

91

tion about past events.

Dialogue, as well as physical action, can provide dramatic tension. To say that at one particular second in their argument Agnes decided to kill Fred is less exciting than listening to some of the words that led to the decision:

> "It's just that . . . you're boring, Agnes. And dull. Dull as a clock."
> "Why don't you just call me stupid and be done with it?"
> "All right! Agnes, you are stupid!"

The reader of this dialogue is now ready for Agnes to reach for the gun.

An exchange can reveal physical description:

> "Fred, you look like a moulting camel," Agnes said.

It not only gives us a glimpse of a character named Fred, but it reveals something of Agnes' personality.

You need to write dialogue that will fit your characters and please both you and your editor. That may take work, but it's not impossible. Once again, it is important to remember that dialogue in fiction is not "real" speech, but with work it can sound as free as an actual conversation. It just takes a bit of conjuring. Our talk is filled with pauses, repetitions, wasted words, intonation, gestures, and all the other paraphernalia humans employ. To convey all that happens in a few scant minutes of actual conversation would take pages of precious space in your book and would be boring to read. What happens simultaneously in reality would require line upon line of print.

Your duty as an author is to become a filter through which the unimportant parts of actual speech are removed before they appear on the page. Good dialogue sounds natural but is not verbatim. This means written speech is often condensed and brief. Few people in real life say more than a few words at a time or get a chance to. Perhaps you have seen contests asking one to complete a statement about a product in twenty-five words or less. Twenty-five words or less is not a bad gauge for fictional dialogue for young adults.

ON THE PAGE

On the printed page, people may interrupt each other, but they cannot talk at the same time. Each speaker must have his own paragraph. Each time you switch speakers, you start a new paragraph. That paragraph may contain not only the actual words spoken, but also any actions or thoughts that belong to that character. Even if your characters speak only in monosyllables, they still need a paragraph each:

> "Yes," Fred said.
> "No!" Agnes replied.

Not only will your readers need clear paragraphing to signal the switch between and among speakers, but they must also clearly and quickly understand WHO is speaking. Those signals are *attributives* or tag lines or "he said's" or anything else you choose to call them. These serve the same purpose as the line in a cartoon which points from the character's mouth to the words lettered above his head in a balloon. At their best, tags are as unobtrusive yet as clear as cartoon conversation pointers. The less noticeable they are, the better. Check your own reading to see how quickly your eyes flit over the "he said's."

Probably the most innocuous way of dealing with attributives is the simplest: "he said," "I said," "Margaret said." Repetitious and dull, you may say. Not really. Most of the time, in most of life, people simply say things. They seldom *declaim, assert, shout,* or *aver.* They simply *say.* Remember, the purpose here is only to identify the speaker. After that the reader is totally concerned with the words being spoken. Incidentally, the moment you make the rather poetic inversion—*said Margaret, said he, said I*—you have taken attention away from the dialogue. And those *saids* do not have to appear like beats of a metronome. The words *are* movable!

> "I'm glad you won the lottery. You deserve every penny," he said.
> "I'm glad you won the lottery," he said. "You deserve every penny."

He looked at me and said, "I'm glad you won the lottery. You deserve every penny."

A simple variation from tag lines is to use a proper name—June, Alex, Rover—instead of the personal pronoun. What you want is clarity, not just repetition. Or if there are only two people involved in a conversation, if their identities are clearly established, you may be able to do without attributes for a while, letting what is *being said* identify the speaker.

Another way to deal with tag lines is to use character action rather than the attributive:

> "How're you doing?" Fred closed the door and leaned against the car.

This not only clues the reader in on who is speaking, but it provides movement and may even indicate that Fred usually approaches any conflict with nonchalance. Care must be taken here that you are not providing so many stage directions—movement, gesture, action—that Fred appears to be a puppet on a string being jerked about the scene. Also beware of any action, logically visualized that becomes ludicrous:

> She dropped her eyes. (One wonders if they broke.)
> He tossed his head. (Did anyone catch it?)
> She threw him a despairing look.
> Her eyes flitted around the room.
> She threw up her hands.

Do avoid tacking on adverbs, the "ly" words, to your attributives in an attempt to tell your reader how your character is speaking: shouted bravely, screamed loudly, murmured softly, tiptoed daintily, grasped greedily. As you can see, such adverbs are redundant. Can one tiptoe without being dainty? Can one really murmur any way but softly? You can also apply pure logic to such a passage as

> "How are you?" Fred asked.

It is obvious Fred asked because what he said was a question. This can be remedied by using a name or dropping the tag entirely or providing a stage direction for Fred. And of course, if you have two people who know each other well and are the only two people in the scene, there is no reason to use the other's name each time one or the other speaks.

PUNCTUATION OF DIALOGUE

In real life conversation, human beings communicate perfectly well without considering punctuation marks, but authors must think punctuation when they put speech to paper. Such marks are merely amenities provided by the author to the reader for clarity. If the rules of punctuation you learned in sixth grade have faded from your memory, all you have to do is pick up a published novel and see how the author handled direct quotations.

A general rule is that exact speech is set off with quotation marks (" "). Indirect quotation is not.

> "I don't want to go," Jane said. Direct Quotation
> Jane said that she didn't want to go. Indirect Quotation
> Note the addition of the word *that*, the change of the personal pronoun from *I* to *she*, and the change of the verb *don't* to *didn't* in order to make the quotation indirect.

Punctuation of direct quotations depends upon the placement of attributives. *One-Sentence Quotes:* If Fred speaks only one sentence or only one word, it is transcribed onto the page thus:

> "I wish she were here to defend me," Fred said.

Note the placement of the comma after the complete sentence spoken by Fred and also the placement of the comma *inside* the quotation mark. The period for the sentence comes at the end of your attributive.

Interrupted One-Sentence Quote: If the attributive interrupts the spoken sentence, it is written thus:

> "If you don't mind," Fred said, "I'd like to join you."

Two-Sentence Quote: If your character says two sentences interrupted by a "he said," it is punctuated in this manner:

> "We have no flights out today," the agent said. "Tomorrow there are three."

Whole Paragraph Speech: In the course of your story one character may go off on a long diatribe. The entire paragraph is then enclosed in quotation marks, *not* each individual sentence.

Two or More Paragraph Speech: In some cases, your character may be retelling an incident that will go on for two or three uninterrupted paragraphs. In this case quotation marks appear at the first of the first paragraph but *not* at the end of the paragraph. At the beginning of the second paragraph, place quotation marks, but do *not* place any at the end. In other words, do not shut off his story with quotation marks but leave his paragraph open for more. Only when the speech is finished do you insert the final quotation marks. However, a good rule is to keep your character from monopolizing the conversation so that he goes on at great length without interruption. It is no more interesting reading than listening to a person who monopolizes an actual conversation.

Broken-Off Sentence: One of your characters may break off in the middle of a sentence. In this case you use ellipsis in this manner:

> "I'm not so sure, but . . .," Fred said.

or

> Fred turned away. "I'm not so sure, but. . . ."

Three dots make up the ellipsis denoting the unspoken words. Use a comma if an attributive follows or a period at the end of the ellipsis if your tag line precedes the incomplete sentence. Notice in the latter case one uses four dots: three for the ellipsis and one for the period. If your character, instead of trailing off into ellipsis, breaks off abruptly, use dashes.

Quotations Within Quotations: The basic rule among American publishers is that a quote within a quote is set off by single quotation marks (').

> "Yes," Agnes said, "I heard him call me 'The Big Oaf.' "

Notice the closing of the single quote and the double marks at the end of the sentence.

CHARACTER THOUGHTS

In fiction, characters should not necessarily keep their thoughts to themselves, although in real life we are often so advised. The problem arises as to how to express, differentiate, and punctuate thoughts on paper. One could say:

> "I should not have said that," she thought.

This only adds another attributive to be juggled, but at least it didn't say "she thought to herself." To whom else would she think? One method of avoiding the "she thoughts" is to change personal pronouns and bravely write out the thought:

> "Drop dead!" she muttered. She shouldn't have said that. She knew very well as soon as the words were out.

The reader knows instantly that the last two sentences were Agnes' thoughts just before she reached for the gun.

Thoughts can also be expressed in italics, which tends to give them added emphasis whether that is intended or not. For young readers, italics can be confusing. For authors, it can reveal a dependence on type face rather than language usage to carry a signal of attribution.

PURPOSE OF DIALOGUE

The mechanics of *how* to write dialogue are important because they facilitate the reader's understanding. Equally important is *what* is being said. In real life, we waste words without thinking: How are you? How's it going? How have you been? Have a good day. Hot enough for you? All of these are mindless ways of easing in or out of conversations. On the printed page such inanities take up too much precious space. Of course not everything your characters say will have deep, complex meaning, but conversation must have some definite purpose.

Dialogue Used to Create Character

Some sage once remarked, "What you ARE speaks so loudly I can't hear what you say." This, in reality, is what writers strive for: to imply obliquely the character and personality of the person speaking. The language in which characters express themselves reveals age, education, ethnic background, geographic area as well as personality and character. What a character says must be so individual that no other person in your story could possibly say the same thing. This keeps your characters from all talking alike. When you are devising speech for characters, say our put-upon Agnes, you as a writer must identify dramatically with Agnes or become the supercilious Fred, who looks like a moulting camel in his professorial tweeds. So individualistic must each speech be that if you were to eliminate all your attributives, the reader would still know who was saying what.

Sometimes it helps a beginning writer to envision the scene and dialogue as part of a one-act play being performed on stage. In a matter of minutes, an actor must appear on stage and convince the audience of his personality, character, and intentions. So the characters in your novel, with only a minimum of stage directions and attributives, must establish themselves as interesting individuals by what they say. After all, you are creating a person who has never lived before and you are creating a way of speaking that is individual to him.

Unless you are the reincarnation of Mark Twain, don't resort to a heavy dose of dialect to create character. First, it is very difficult to write correctly and consistently; second, it is usually equally difficult to read. All too often, what is meant as regional or ethnic speech comes out as parody, sometimes embarrassing, sometimes insulting.

However, it is possible to create the illusion of ethnic speech by concentrating on the rhythm of the sentences, the order of the words with only an occasional word that might be associated with dialect, whether regional or ethnic. In presenting a fictional account in *We Are Mesquakie We Are One* of the Mesquakie resistance to white civilization in the early 1800s, Hadley Irwin used this technique:

> Gray Gull stopped where our bark lodge had stood and said, "We go no farther."
> "Why, Grandmother?"
> She pointed toward the fields. Around our fields stood the White Ones' fences. And where our seeds had been buried were only empty holes like open graves.
> "We will starve," I said.
> "We will live. Nuts lie beneath the melting snow. Fish move under the ice. Geese and ducks will soon return. When hunger gnaws we chew the bark of slippery elm."
> I was hungry. All were hungry. We did not starve.

You can lend the flavor of dialect without resorting to misspellings and hard to read mispronunciations by inserting an occasional ethnic, foreign, or idiomatic word into the dialogue. Such words will probably appear in italics in your published book and, with the added emphasis, will successfully suggest dialect. If you are not personally and deeply familiar with speech other than standard American English, you might do well to seek out the help of a member of the group whose speech you want to use— for a reading fee, of course!

Another aspect of conversation that you will want to consider is the use of slang, profanity, or even obscenity. Slang is a constant in most teenagers' vocabularies, but it changes so quickly that the last year's "humongous" or "gross" may sound archaic by the time your book is in print. Use slang sparingly. Use it in the context of the time and place upon which you are focusing and hope for the best. The question of profanity/obscenity and the often resulting censorship will be with us always. There is no real solution. One quick walk through the halls of any junior high or high school between classes will assure you that few words are unfamiliar to your potential readers. And yes, honesty and realism are important in a novel. You might, however, as a beginning writer for young adults, consider two suggestions: *When in doubt, cut it out. Less is more.*

Dialogue Used to Reveal Relationships

An author always has the choice of whether to tell or to show, to summarize or dramatize. Can you remember, however, when you were a teenager skipping over descriptive and expository passages to "get on with the story?" Young readers still enjoy scenes where people talk. Besides enjoyment, however, young readers, through dialogue, learn to create a character along with an author, to imagine feelings, and to infer relationships. How much more interesting for a teenager to read:

> "Chip Martin! Would you mind combing your hair? Just once. And let me trim it there in front," Mom suggested as I sprawled across the sofa. "You're going to ruin your eyes trying to squint through that mop."
> "Get off my back, will you? What's wrong with my hair? I'm just letting it grow natural."

rather than

> When I was in the eighth grade, I argued with Mom all the time because she seemed to do nothing but criticize me and I guess I felt like being mean to her.

Conversation that illustrates but does not tell, that implies but does not state such human relationships and feelings as jealousy, envy, admiration, and dislike forces young readers to draw their own conclusions and make their own discoveries about characters.

Dialogue to Advance the Plot

Fast-paced dialogue moves a plot ahead and keeps a reader turning the page. What better way to foreshadow events and create suspense than to HEAR not only a protagonist's fear and suspicions but also the reaction of the antagonist? If the recommended point, according to the ancient Greeks is to begin a story *in medias res* (in the middle of things), then one interesting way to fill a reader in on past events or necessary background is by dialogue, deftly handled so that the author's manipulative footprints are neatly covered.

Through dialogue an author can employ dramatic irony: letting the reader know something that a character cannot know, and thus creating wonder on the part of the reader as to how the character will discover this information.

The visual impact of conversation can work to your advantage in terms of the pace of your book. Because of paragraphing and the amount of white space, a page of dialogue reads faster than a page of narration or exposition. Certainly as you approach the climax and conclusion of your story, you will choose scene and dialogue. Perhaps every good tale embodies a sense of mystery. Pick up a mystery novel and read the final chapter. Seldom is the solution couched in exposition. Instead the characters TALK. And again, in order to maintain the illusion of a fast pace, keep the length of characters' speeches under control. After all, few of us other than teachers, lawyers, politicians, and preachers have the chance to orate at length.

Finally, after all the pitfalls and problems and challenges of writing dialogue, there is a marvelous bonus. Those lovely, funny, witty lines that you've been dying to use, but which would be author intrusion anywhere else, can emerge whole and unobtrusively from the mouth of your most delightful character.

·nine·

MIDDLES— USING PRIME TIME

◆——————◆

Brian, a student in a fiction class, had an excellent idea for a YA novel and he had the writing skills he needed. Of course, both he and the instructor realized that as a full-time college student, Brian couldn't complete the novel within the limits of one semester, but he could certainly make a good start.

The beginning chapters, some sixty pages, were promising. By the last month of the term, three central characters were firmly established, point of view had been settled, the tone of the writing in the voice of a first person narrator was clear and individual.

Brian even knew how the book would end. In the last weeks of the semester, he wrote the two final chapters that would bring the story to a satisfying conclusion.

Only one real problem remained—the missing ninety-plus pages that would form the center and heart of the book. What Brian needed were the intermediate events that would hold a reader's attention.

IT'S A PLOT

Many authors in the throes of writing their first book find palms growing moist, stomachs turning queasy, and little beads of sweat breaking out on their brows at the very mention of the word *plot*. In their minds it conjures dark dealings, huddled figures, connivings, twistings and turnings, and characters who are up to no good. *Their* novels, they say, have none of these ingredients. They are afraid of plots.

Not to worry. Plot is conflict stemming from obstacles a character meets in the process of the story. Plot develops through a character's participation in a series of motivated incidents that affect the growth of the main characters. Plot is not a complete structural narrative with characters inserted to provide the action. Plot is organic, growing naturally from the cause and effect of events involving character.

Defining plot is much easier than the actual plotting, but you can make a game of it, a game of *what if*. It can become as delightful a pastime as day-dreaming out on your patio on a sunny day; in fact, such a relaxed setting is ideal. You may start by thinking of your main character and wondering, "What if. . . ." What if Jesse has been termed incorrigible by his parents and has been sent to spend a year with his grandfather on a midwestern farm? What if Jesse hates the farm, so different from the surfing life he had known in California? What if he runs away? What if he doesn't run away? Don't accept the usual answer to your question. Go for the logical, but not the obvious. Think of alternative actions and the complications they might entail.

A key word is *complications*. The protagonist must not find life easy. Whether the girl in your novel is searching for the mother who abandoned her at birth, is seeking acceptance by a peer group, is working for a desperately coveted scholarship, is trying to lick addiction to drugs or alcohol, or is finding true love—obstacles will arise that make attaining the goal a matter of real concern. The character may or may not win out, but the end must be logical, consistent with problems in the story, and supportive of the point on which your novel is based. Whatever the outcome, the plot is the glue that holds your story together.

Trollope did not use the word *plot,* but he said:

> I have from the first felt sure that the writer when he sits down to commence his novel, should do so not because he *has* to tell a story, but because he has a story to tell. The novelist's first

novel will generally have sprung from the right cause. Some series of events, or some development of character, will have presented itself to his imagination—and this he feels so strongly that he thinks he can present his picture in strong and agreeable language to others. He sits down and *tells* his story because he has a story to *tell*; as you, my friend, when you have heard something which at once tickled your fancy or moved your pathos, will hurry to tell it to the first person you meet.

CAUSE AND EFFECT

E. M. Forster, in *Aspects of the Novel,* tells us that a story answers "and then" and plot answers "why." He illustrates this by defining a story as "The King died and then the Queen died." Plot, he says, is "The King died and the Queen died of grief." The first is merely chronological. The second is cause and effect.

Life has no plot. Life is a jig-saw puzzle that leaves humans wondering how the pieces fit. An author makes order from this chaos by building scene upon scene of conflict up to a point-of-no-return, the climax, and then rushes on to the solution in what is termed the falling action. Like a chain, when one link of a plot is weak, the entire chain or story becomes useless. When one scene does not add to or advance the conflict, the entire plot can fail.

One link that can weaken the plot is the use of coincidence. A novelist is allowed one coincidence at the beginning of the story, e.g., coincidentally, your protagonist and antagonist may be in the same place at the same time in order to provide an opening scene of the conflict. After that the writer must rely on cause and effect.

A writer was once told of a strange coincidence that occurred in her family. An aunt and uncle adopted a child, knowing at the time the identity of the natural mother. Through the years, the aunt kept track of the boy's natural mother. When the adopted son was in college, he wrote home to invite his adopted mother to come on campus and meet his best friend. When the mother was introduced to the friend, she discovered it was her adopted son's half brother. Interestingly enough, she never told her son of the relationship. In this case, life was too coincidental to include in a story and attempting to translate this incident into a believable plot would appear to the critical reader as manipulation. The Greeks called such manipulation *deus ex machina,* a god lowered to the stage by machine to make things right.

COMPLICATIONS AND SUBPLOTS: ATTENTION THROUGH TENSION

Significant action begins a story; conflicts and resolutions are the bases of plot; suspense keeps the reader's interest. Complications and subplots are the means by which you can develop intermediate crises; they offer ways of building drama and tension while adding to, not detracting from, the central conflict of the story. In fiction as in reality, the shortest distance between two points may be a straight line, but it's not necessarily the most interesting route. Detours can be fascinating.

An excellent example of *complications* used to build tension and provide intermediate crises is *The Power of the Rellard* by Carolyn F. Logan.

The *story line* involves three children, Shelley, Georgie, and Lucy, who invent a game which turns into reality. It is a tale of the battle between good and evil, between the power of the Rellard and the forces of darkness.

The *plot* begins with *significant events*—Lucy returns from the hospital with a withered hand after an illness and the children are given a toy theater by their mother. The *basic conflict* arises when a cardboard doll, Rellard, becomes, in their game, a make-believe source of power, and then as the story progresses, the power is no longer imagined, but becomes real.

The *complications* are varied and grow in intensity as the book moves forward. They include a contest among the children to decide who will wield the power, discoveries about what the power can do, confrontations with forces which would destroy both the power and the children. Each crisis adds suspense to the story, each contributes to the central conflict between good and evil, each is resolved as the narrative unfolds. Yet it is not until the *climax* of the story that the final confrontation occurs and the contest between light and darkness is decided. Then comes the *dénouement,* the winding down of the action, the wrapping up of details including the healing of Lucy's hand.

If complications build plot, *subplots* can add richness and depth to your story. A subplot consists of a series of events that have a slightly different focus from the main plot, but occur within the same time frame and involve characters who are part of the central story.

As you commit your novel to paper, the makings of a subplot may begin to develop without your knowlege. If this happens it's like a gift. When Eyerly invented the police officer in *If I Loved You Wednesday* who confronted the love-sick Dennis outside the apartment of his beloved Ms. Carr, he was only that, a police officer. Not until many chapters later did the writer discover he wasn't a policeman at all, but rather a sociologist studying police methods and criminal behavior. Imagine her delight when later still she realized he would fall in love and marry the object of Dennis's affection.

Of course, not all subplots arise as a bit of surprise to the author, but no matter whether spontaneous or carefully planned in advance, to be successful, they develop through character and specific circumstance rather than being simple digressions.

Occasionally, the central character may be involved in a subplot; that is, events may arise that distract your protagonist from his primary goal and temporarily engage his energy. In Carol J. Scott's novel, *Kentucky Daughter,* the plot revolves around Mary Fred Pratley's learning to accept, with pride, her family heritage and to adapt to life in Virginia with her aunt and uncle. A subplot develops when her English teacher, Mr. Dolsey, makes sexual advances toward her, creating a situation that must be resolved before she can get on with her life and plans.

A different sort of subplot occurs in Hadley Irwin's *Abby, My Love.* Although the story is based on Chip's growing love for Abby and his eventual discovery that she is the victim of incest, a subplot develops as his mother becomes romantically involved with an old family friend and must decide whether or not to marry him. In a sense, this secondary story line provides a reflection and variation of the main plot.

Used skillfully, the combination of parts and whole results in an exciting story, a satisfying conclusion, a "good read." Stories can, however, become too complex or too cluttered. Like jugglers with too many balls in the air, authors find they can't handle them all. It may happen that the reader can't handle them either and becomes so confused by plot, subplot, and number of characters that the book is given up in favor of TV.

Devices such as long letters, lengthy excerpts from diaries, or endless retelling of a story-within-a-story are often skipped over by the reader. Such digressions may be due to lazy plotting. No less sloppy is dropping a broad hint as to a future result: "Had I but known" or "Little did Agnes realize that. . . ." These tend to destroy the illusion of reality in your story and focus attention on the author instead of on the characters and the plot.

Skillful, artful fiction depends upon the writer's understanding of the relationship between parts and the whole. It means presenting, via plot and subplots, characters acting in situations that allow the abstract theme of the story to become actual and concrete to the reader. In order to be successful, your story must move.

The basis of narrative is movement through time. The last thing you want is a sense of inertia.

An intrinsic means of providing movement or the illusion of movement is a combination of scene and summary. *Scene* is shared experience, the opportunity for the reader to take part in the action of the story; *summary* is necessary information that does not need dramatization through action and dialogue.

Think of life itself. Most of any day you are probably quite busy *doing* things, encountering people, even talking on the phone. Translated to the page that would be scene. But if you are lucky, there are periods of time when you simply sit and think—about anything. You summarize in your mind what you have done or what you are going to do. Both activities are necessary in living; both are necessary in fiction. Both are natural to and recognizable by your readers.

The difference between scene and summary is exactly the difference between reading a *TV Guide* description of a television program and watching the program itself. The summary is useful; with luck, the program offers more excitement.

The question, then, becomes where do you use scene? Where do you write summary?

SCENE

Start with the premise that you want the entire focus of the book on the characters and what they are up to, not on you, the writer. That means scene will probably play the prominent part in your story and the reader will be sharing the actions, dialogue, and reactions of people in your novel. Your readers will be living the story along with the characters, and in doing so, will become involved in the action. No matter which point of view you have chosen, the elements of scene remain the same; you will use action, dialogue, reaction—anything that creates a sense of immediacy.

Paul Zindel in *My Darling, My Hamburger* uses scene as the opening of the novel. In doing so, he immediately involves the reader in character and action.

> "It was Marie Kazinski who asked how to stop a boy if he wants to go all the way," Maggie whispered.
> Liz dragged her trig book along the wall tiles so it clicked at every crack.
> "I'll bet she didn't ask it like that," Liz said.
> " 'Sexually stimulated' was how she said it, if you must know the sordid details."

In just a few lines of dialogue and action, the reader is given the age and sex of the central characters, as well as what is of current interest to them. Even setting is taken care of via "trig book" and "tiled walls."

The same kind of effect can be achieved without dialogue as Laura Ingalls Wilder shows at the beginning of *On the Banks of Plum Creek*.

> The dim wagon track went no farther on the prairie, and Pa stopped the horses.
> When the wagon wheels stopped turning, Jack dropped down in the shade between them. His belly sank on the grass and his front legs stretched out. His nose fitted in the furry hollow. All of him rested, except his ears.

Whether you use conversation, action or description, or a combination of all three, you are creating scene. Add to those elements the thoughts of a character and the scene takes on another dimension.

In Ouida Sebestyen's *Words by Heart,* the technique works well.

> The first thing Lena saw when she reached the attic behind Mrs. Chism was a stack of books. Then, piles of them, boxes of them, dumped like trash on the floor. "Are all these yours?" she almost whispered in admiration.
>
> "Those? Oh, hell, I took those out of the bookcases when my kids moved away. I needed a place to store my good dishes."
>
> "But—do you come up here to read them?" It was like seeing the pie. Her mouth watered.
>
> In the one-window dimness Mrs. Chism stared at her with no expression on her face. "We'll start in the far corner," she said. "I'm clearing out Gooch's stuff. And the children's stuff. Selling the whole lot. If they wanted it, they should have come got it. A little visit to their own mother wouldn't kill them. I've got grandchildren I haven't even seen."
>
> Lena backed away longingly from the books. She had to ask if she could read them. She had to read them. Even school didn't have half as many, and besides she had read those. But the time didn't seem right. Maybe after she had worked hard and the tightness had left Mrs. Chism's face. . . .

Scene and Summary

There will be times in your writing when you want to convey information or fill in a bit of background, yet you don't want to entirely stop the action of the story. The information will be summary, but it can be written in such a way that it seems a part of your character's thoughts.

Rap, a ten-year-old boy, plays hookey from school in *I Be Somebody* (Hadley Irwin).

> He sat hidden under the willows until he was sure he was safe, wishing all the time he were back in school.
>
> He reached for his jackknife. Aunt Spicy said it used to belong to his granddaddy, but it was still a good knife. The blades

were thin, worn down from honing, the case rough and cold like tree bark in winter and tipped at both ends with brass—real brass. He had learned when he was little how to make a willow whistle. His first one hadn't worked, but Dan Creek had been patient and spent one whole afternoon showing him how.

He chose a switch of willow as big as his thumb and cut. . . .

The authors wanted to supply a little of Rap's past and to foreshadow his relationship with Dan. The question that has always to be answered is, does the reader need to experience the particular moments or can the event be told *about* more efficiently? Here it didn't seem important to sit through the process of Dan's teaching Rap for one long afternoon. It would have taken at least a couple of pages of dialogue to illustrate one word—patience. There would be time later in the book to put Dan and Rap in a scene that would demonstrate their closeness.

In Lynn Hall's *The Shy Ones,* the author makes a similar choice. Robin, the central character, is waking slowly and remembering.

> Last night had been pretty bad. Awful, in fact. Sock hops were supposed to be fun. Casual, happy, everybody dancing and having a ball. Well, she'd gone. Full of optimism, she had walked to the gym with Marilyn and Darlene, checked her loafers at the door with everybody else, and padded on into the streamer-hung basketball court, feeling foolish in her stocking feet.

Here the summary does double duty. It recaps events and feelings and sets up nicely a brief flashback to the dance itself which is also summarized, not written as a complete scene.

What works in third person can work just as well in first person. In *The Lilith Summer,* Ellen, twelve, in order to earn money for a ten-speed bicycle, has agreed to spend the summer with Lilith, a seventy-seven-year-old woman. The authors wanted to convey Ellen's impressions of her first encounter without going step-by-step through the day.

> I ran—that first day—all the way uphill to Farley's cottonwood and didn't slow down until I was nearly home. I breathed

111

through my mouth, trying to get rid of the taste of Lilith's house. It tasted old. It tasted musty. Musty on towels and rugs, on blankets and walls, in bedrooms, in closets, like a mouthful of lake water.

I ran—still seeing the picture in Lilith's bedroom of a wolf on a snowy hill, mouth open, head tipped back with icicles hanging from his jowls, howling at the moon.

I ran—trying to forget the house of Lilith and the clock with a two-pound can of pepper as big as a brick beside it.

I ran because I knew I was caught in the circle of that house for the rest of the summer.

SUMMARY

Occasionally there will be information that is necessary for the reader which does not fit comfortably into dialogue or interior monologue. You may literally need a paragraph or two to present the material. In a sense, when done well, and if ideas are couched in the same language you've been using, the pause will seem just that—a pause, not an interruption.

The third paragraph of Wilder's *On the Banks of Plum Creek* does just this. The reader has already met Jack the dog, knows that the story takes place in a prairie setting, and has a sense of the era because travel is done with horse and wagon. The rest of the background is given in one paragraph of summary.

> All day long for many, many days, Jack had been trotting under the wagon. He had trotted all the way from the little log house in Indian Territory, across Kansas, across Missouri, across Iowa, and a long way into Minnesota. He had learned to take his rest whenever the wagon stopped.

And there it is, neatly done, phrased in the kind of language that will be used throughout the story. We have learned in capsule form most of what we need to know about the past. The rest will come primarily through dialogue or characters' thoughts.

A variation of summary is accomplished by the illusion that the central character, first person point of view, is speaking directly to the reader. That's the case in S. E. Hinton's *That Was Then, This Is Now.*

112

> Mark and me went down to the bar/pool hall about two or three blocks from where we lived with the sole intention of making some money. We'd done that before. I was a really good pool player, especially for being just sixteen years old, and, what's more, I looked like a baby-faced kid who wouldn't know one ball from another. This, and the way Mark set me up, helped me hustle a lot of pool games. The bad deal is, it's against the law to be in this pool hall if you're under age, because of the adjoining bar.

The reader has been given what amounts to a brief biography, yet the effect is perfectly natural and creates a feeling of intimacy. The rules for using summary are simple: don't stop your story; don't let the author's voice intrude. What worked for Herman Melville in *Moby Dick* probably won't work in a YA book. A lot of readers have found it disconcerting, while caught up in Ahab's mad search for the white whale, to run headlong into all that information, accurate though it was, about the intricacies of turning whales into blubber, meat and oil.

DESCRIPTION

In the foregoing examples you probably noticed the use of description in both scene and summary. Description is another element that can change the sense of time or movement in your writing. Just as you probably would never use a whole page of summary, neither would you use an entire page of description. The key to proportion is this: everything you write—scene, dialogue, summary, description—must contribute directly to the movement of the plot. Nothing is wasted, but over-writing will cause your reader to lose interest.

Specificity is as important in writing description as it is in writing a "how to" article for a magazine. However, being specific does not mean a string of adjectives or adverbs; more likely it means saying "elm" instead of "tree," "brass" instead of "metal," or "two-pound" can rather than "large" can. Aim to make every sentence paint a picture.

Remember, when writing description, that you and your reader have more senses than one. Most of us respond most quickly to visual images, but depending on only that one, you have left out the other five: smell, sound, touch, taste, and the wonderful things that can be done with kinesthetic images. Of course you would never use all of the sense impressions in a single paragraph any more than you would deliberately choose to write a passage of description that depended on a particular one. But the range is there to be made use of. In descriptive writing, just as in summary in general, the voice, the words, the perceptions, the attitudes should be those of the character about whom you are writing.

CLICHÉS

Lazy language—clichés or overworked, hackneyed expressions—can kill your book. When words spring forth in ready-made clumps, chances are you have just written a series of metaphors that have long lost their freshness and appeal. "Sly as a fox," "quick as a wink," "straight as an arrow"—the list is endless. What you are actually doing with the use of such tired expressions is insulting the intelligence of your young readers or, if you will, stereotyping your audience.

Sometimes you may not even be aware that the metaphor you have coined is, in truth, a cliché. In such a case, find a well-read friend who will be able to spot the offender immediately. However, some clichés are so old they are meaningless ("tough as rawhide") or so ancient they are illogical ("clean as a whistle") or so popular they are worn out ("never having to say you're sorry").

If a phrase sounds familiar to you, it's probably stale. Toss it out and invent something fresh and vivid.

IT'S GOOD BUT WILL THEY TURN THE PAGE?

Even with the plot firmly in mind, characters who speak and act like living persons, and a clear understanding of the workings of scene and summary, something can go wrong. To prove the point, ask any roomful of junior high students if they've ever started reading a book and not finished it and immediately hands will start waving. Questioned as to what turned them off, they will present you with vague answers. "Boring," yawns a lanky fourteen-year-old boy. "Too much description," says a girl across the aisle. A more articulate student volunteers, "I couldn't relate to it." Whatever the answer, the reader of that particular book didn't have enough interest in the story to turn the page.

Our early ancestors, the cave dwellers, handled the problem summarily. Sitting around the campfire, worn out from hunting the woolly mammoth or hairy rhinoceros, if anyone fell asleep or guessed the ending as the clan story teller droned on and on, they killed the story teller.

This need not happen to you. A four letter word called *pace*, ranking right up there with the four-letter word *plot*, makes all the difference. Pamela Frankau's definition in her *Pen To Paper, A Novelist's Notebook* comes close to explaining the importance of this abstraction. She writes that pace is what "makes a good story better." Pacing is to fiction as rhythm is to music. Pacing can create mood, control a reader's interest and emotional response, supply irony or shock value, produce comedy, enhance tragedy, create a rise and fall of tension and evoke a sense of immediacy.

STRUCTURAL PACING DEVICES

Start your novel with a bang, with a brass band, with a leap into the action, avoiding clumps of explanation and description. There will be time to sprinkle in such information later after you have securely hooked your young reader. Set up clearly, in these opening scenes, the problem for your protagonist to face and for your reader to worry about. A worried reader is an involved reader.

In *Kim/Kimi*, Hadley Irwin begins the story with a confrontation between Kim and Miss Strum, the high school principal (the leap into action). The author then reveals through actual conversation interspersed with Kim's thoughts that Kim has walked out of Mr. Mitchell's history class because a film about Pearl Harbor was being shown and that Kim Andrews is really Kimi Yogushi, half Japanese (no long explanations and little description). The reader discovers that the problem facing Kim is her "difference" from her classmates (problem for protagonist to face).

Now is the time in the story, after this rather intense opening scene with the principal, to relax things a bit, introduce basic characters, and suggest a means of Kim's solving her problem. This pause in the plot allows readers to catch their breaths before encountering the next development. The trick here is to provide all the necessary information about Kim's immediate family without slowing the action and at the same time to arouse the reader's curiosity concerning Kim's real Japanese-American father, who died before she was born. All this is accomplished by means of dialogue, a brief flashback, immediate action, and Kim's thoughts.

Build from crisis to crisis, complication to complication for the remainder of the book in short brisk scenes that propel the reader forward. Try to avoid having all your scenes the same length, and you will also want to vary the emotional intensity, even mixing elements of comedy with more serious matters. What the scenes consist of, of course, depends upon your particular story.

During Kim's stay in Sacramento, the scenes consist of her encounters with various characters who help her in her search for her Japanese family. Some of these meetings are only casual; others result in lasting relationships. The pacing is built on Kim's successes and failures as she continues her quest. In the course of her adventure, she discovers the different facets of Japaneseness; but neither Kimi nor her reader are confident of her success.

Pacing is always slowed by aggregate clumps of anything: scenes, summaries, descriptions, exposition, dialogue. Unfortunately, there is no ratio, no formula in arriving at a magic balance that makes for good pacing. Fortunately, good editors exist who are adept at spotting the rushed scenes as well as the lack of movement. Unfortunately, editorial help arrives only after the book's written. You must become your own good editor, spotting the too-slow and the too-fast and making adjustments until you've achieved a steady, brisk pace throughout.

Generate interest by having a character work against time to achieve or prevent something. Allow readers to look forward to a specific event or confrontation by letting them know, before it happens, that it's coming. Your reader must be inspired to ask,

"What will happen next?" Pacing is also enhanced by placing your character in a dilemma where she must choose between either two desirable or less than desirable alternatives.

Kimi has less than a week to find her father's family, so time is a determining factor in the pacing of *Kim/Kimi*. Throughout her search, she is aware of upcoming possibilities that she will have to encounter which may or may not aid her when they occur. Her dilemmas are threefold: Should she stay in California and continue looking or should she give up and go home? If she finds her father's family, should she attempt to meet them or should she be satisfied in knowing they exist? If she meets her family, will they accept her or reject her?

Enhance the plot by a reversal of what your reader or your central character might suspect or by a surprise, if the surprise has been legitimized by ample motivation. Move the plot along by summarizing events which obviously have to take place, but do not add to the story's forward drive—things like getting up each morning, eating breakfast, getting dressed, and so on.

In *Kim/Kimi*, a reversal occurs when best friend Jav turns up in Sacramento and reveals that Kim's parents have been totally aware of where she is and what she has been doing. A surprise, the groundwork for which has been carefully laid, happens when Kim discovers that a marriage had been arranged between her father and a sister of the woman who had been helping Kimi in her search. Of course Hadley Irwin omitted recounting such details as when Kim fell asleep, what she had for breakfast, and all other such mundane details. Focusing on the important keeps away narrative clutter and makes readers ask, "How will all of this turn out?"

Satisfy the reader with an ending that is neither too long nor too short. A well-paced ending should suggest to the reader that the story line goes on after the book is finished and leaves the reader wishing there were a sequel, yet feeling that *this* segment of life is over for the time being. *Kim/Kimi* consists of 200 pages; the final scene is seven pages long. This ratio is by no means prescriptive, but that proportion and that pacing worked for this particular book.

In this final scene, Kimi meets her aunt and her grandmother for the second time, feels reconciled to her aunt, and is rejected by her Japanese grandmother. Then she discovers that the seeming rejection is only an unspoken plea:

> "Your grandmother says she needs time. Time to understand the past. Time to think about the future and her Kimiko."
> "Kimiko?"
> "It means 'her child Kimi.' It means you are family."

Organic or structural pacing certainly depends on the interaction of scene and summary, on the use of plot complications, but another element of pacing is in the text itself, that is, the actual words on the page. This means eliminating or rewriting any sentences that require rereading in order to clarify meaning or sequence of events.

Reading suspect sections of your novel aloud is fine if you have a listener, but it works almost as well without an audience and is probably the surest way to find out if the pace of your novel is slowing. Skipping or wishing you could skip sentences or even paragraphs as you read, so you can get to the "good" part, is a certain sign of slow reading. As you read, listen to your sentences. Are some of them too long? Too tangled? Do you find that even you have trouble putting all the commas in the right places? Do all the sentences seem to be monotonous? Are they all the same length? If so, vary them. Sometimes two words can take the place of two dozen. Do you find when reading it aloud that the paragraph of description over which you labored so lovingly for half a morning is faintly boring? Do certain scenes go on too long? Pamela Frankau puts it bluntly when she writes:

> Every scene has a natural end to it. When the end comes, it must guard against elaboration . . . an artificial wind-off. There needs no thunderous chord struck, no pointed little comment. "And he strode from the room." The curtain can come down on a spoken question that doesn't get an answer. I can, if I have done right by the scene, leave them (the characters) all standing just as they are. In the shifting of the scene, pace is essential—and easy, once you learn you can get them up stairs without mentioning the stairs.

Frankau also says that an almost certain sign that the pace is dragging is her own mental attitude that she has "a feeling of boredom or dullness of spirit."

Sometimes lack of pace is attributable to something other than length, description, or dragged-out unnecessary scenes. If this should be the case, the fault may be the foundation on which you are erecting the whole structure of your novel. You may be trying to begin too early, or too late, in the story line. Or a subplot may be trying to take over everything. Or you may have written your story into a corner, with no way to escape except backing up and heading in some wholly new direction. To find where the fault is, and here we are speaking almost geologically, takes an almost scientific detachment and a probable rewrite. When a story bogs down, the best way to move ahead may be to go back, rethink, and make a fresh start.

CHAPTERS

Just as the use of scene and summary is a means of pacing your story by creating tension and excitement for your reader, so too can divisions create movement.

Certainly, a book can be written in which there are no divisions, in which the story flows directly from page 1 to page 250 with no formal breaks or stops; however, few young readers have the time to read your book at one sitting. At least for the convenience of the reader and to create a sense of discovery, chapters are useful.

Chapter divisions round out a scene and provide readers time to take a breath after the climax of one event and before encountering another conflict. You will also find that chapters allow you as an author to pass over some unimportant time spans. They can provide an overall symmetry to the pattern of your book. In *The Pigman* (Zindel) chapters denote a change in narrator as the story is told alternately by John and Lorraine.

Many writers, including Charles Dickens, published first in magazines, a chapter at a time—emphasizing the notion that each chapter, in a sense, was entire unto itself, yet urged the reader forward. The use of chapters demands careful attention to the last lines because they have to be satisfying in themselves yet at the same time they must make the reader wonder what happens next. An obvious use of such technique was "Who shot JR?" which carried the interest in the TV series "Dallas" through an entire summer. Not that you would write an actual question as the last sentence of the chapter, but the question might well be implicit as in *Abby, My Love* (Hadley Irwin):

> The phone woke me—it must have been after midnight. At first I thought it was some kind of joke. All I heard was somebody breathing. I was ready to hang up when Abby spoke. She didn't speak exactly, she whispered.
> "Meet me in the park tomorrow afternoon. Please. I need to talk to you. Chip, I'm scared."
> I didn't have a chance to answer before she hung up.

Whether to title or number your chapters will be another decision you will have to make. If your book is divided into fifteen chapters, it will mean you will have to think up fifteen titles to catch the reader's interest and yet not give away the contents of the chapter. It is probably too much to ask; however, it might be a technique to use in the process of your writing to keep you from digressing in time or setting or plot. You may find, after you have finished your story, that such titles are intrusive and that simple numbering works better.

But if you have a knack for caption writing, provocative chapter titles are a good way to lead the reader from one chapter into the next and thus contribute to the feeling that the plot is speeding toward its destination. Long or short, it doesn't matter just so they serve this purpose. One and two-word headings such as "Wheels," "Making Out," "Loverbird," "Jettisoned," and "Surprise" worked well in *He's My Baby, Now* (Eyerly) because all the chapters were short, some less than a page.

VARIATIONS

A.A. Milne in his classic *Winnie the Pooh* uses chapter titles which absolutely describe the contents of the chapter: "Chapter One in which we are introduced to Winnie the Pooh. . . ."

It works because the book is episodic in nature, each chapter being equivalent to a short story. In this kind of novel you offer the reader a series of episodes, each complete in itself. These events do not necessarily have a cause and effect relationship, but rather they are connected because they occur in chronological order to a single character.

This structure has a long and distinguished history as the picaresque novel in all of its infinite variations from *Don Quixote* through *Huckleberry Finn.* It can work equally well in contemporary Young Adult books.

Chunks

If the notion of chapters appears too jumpy, but you still want divisions of some sort, your story can be divided into sections by seasons, settings, time spans, or stages of character growth. In *Moon and Me* (Hadley Irwin) the authors used variations of the title of the book to label sections which displayed changes in the attitude of one of the central characters: *Moonrise. Moonlight. Moonbeam.*

It might be useful to think of sections as acts in a play or movements in a symphony, each pleasing in itself but always contributing to the impact of the whole. You may find that you will begin writing with chapters in mind, but that the length of the chapters vary too greatly to be aesthetically satisfying. Perhaps the story itself is telling you that it belongs in chunks, not chapters. Whether you are talking about chapters or sections, the length as well as the kind of division should be dictated by your overall purpose.

In writing, as well as in architecture, *form* follows *function.*

Visualize the Page

Pace has its visual as well as its practical aspects. Not all young people are born readers. They not only have to be hooked at the outset, but their interest has to be maintained throughout the 25,000 to 40,000 or more words of your story. The dense look of a page with large blocks of type unbroken by dialogue, with too-long paragraphs or chapters that seem to have no end can bring the reader to a halt.

There's a lesson here. If a paragraph or chapter looks too long, see if there is some way you can tighten or condense it. Use dialogue between characters to give the reader needed information instead of imparting it through long sections of exposition.

The Last Word

Remember, it was not on description or characterization that Scheherezade, that remarkable storyteller, relied when she was doing her best to keep her husband from chopping off her head. One smart lady, she ended each night's tale by stopping in the middle of an exciting sentence just as the sun began to rise. You need not go this far, but it is something to bear in mind.

Its name is plot and its first cousin's name is pace.

ten

HOW TO GET FROM THE HOUSE TO THE BARN

One author, upon being asked how the writing was progressing, answered, "Terrible! I'm stuck. I can't get from the house to the barn." The problem appears to be a simple one. The character is in the house and must go to the barn for the next incident. But how does the writer motivate and move the character to the barn without accompanying him step by step?

Unless a novel is going to be a simple narrative, transitions can be a problem. Spelled out, this means how you manage the passage of time in your novel without boring your readers with endless details that do nothing to advance the story. Even the business of moving a character from one day to the next or one place to another can provide a strong temptation to walk with her as she comes home from school, eats dinner, goes to bed, gets up and goes to school where, we can but hope, the real story is going to take up again.

Following this circuitous route is hazardous. 1) Your reader is apt to stop reading and 2) you may become so bogged down that you may stop writing.

The Transition Solution, however, is simple. Whether you want to skip ahead a few hours, a day, a weekend or a week, all you have to do is *tell* the reader that *that amount of time has elapsed.*

After all, you are the one writing this story. You are the boss.

A device we call the Flea Hop makes transitions easy for you and the reader. Usually used within the confines of a single chapter, it consists of merely rolling off an extra space or two on your typewriter, regardless of what preceded it, and picking up the story at the very point you want to be, presumably when something interesting is about to happen.

The following three examples, each with a different time frame, tell the reader that nothing worth mentioning happened in the periods indicated:

> *Two days passed* before Robin summoned the courage to make the telephone call. Then pity for Cass won out.
>
> *The weekend* dragged by and on Monday, Robin, against her own judgment, went looking for Brew.
>
> Stephanie's *diet lasted two weeks* and in the entire time she had not spoken a civil word to anyone until the day she bumped into Fritz in the laundromat.

In addition to building a bridge over time, Flea Hops can enrich your story. A clause strategically inserted can add a new dimension, favorable or unfavorable, to a chapter or prepare the reader for a later development in the plot.

> *Except for a knock-down and drag-out fight with Elaine* over whose turn it was to do the dishes—*the fight ended in a draw*—*the week-end* was such a drag that Kate was glad when Monday came.

A Flea Hop can also let you introduce a new character, perhaps one you don't even know you'll need. The Mr. Hooper in the following example may never be mentioned again, or he might serve a useful purpose ten chapters later on.

> Day after day went by and finally, after *two weeks* of waiting, during which time Laura was sure she would never hear from Chris again—the mailman dropped a fat, official-looking envelope into the mailbox the Ferrises shared with Mr. Hooper, who lived in the other half of the duplex.

In the first example we pass over an uninteresting weekend and at the same time give evidence of a family feud that has only been hinted at before. In the second example, the reader is allowed to skip nimbly over two weeks in which there were only two things worth reporting: that Chris was about to appear in Laura's life again and that Mr. Hooper lives in the other half of the duplex. You will be pleasantly surprised when you find out how handy a Mr. Hooper, who uninvited stepped into your story, can be.

This happened in *Someone to Love Me* (Eyerly). Mrs. Fawcett, otherwise known as Madame Galaxy, was introduced into the story merely as a nosy neighbor but grew so interesting that she became a pivotal part of the novel. The author does not know what she would have done without her.

Variations on the Flea Hop are endless and can be tailored to any situation where any period of time, long or short, should lightly be skipped over. All are equally effective whether used internally, i.e., within a chapter, to end a chapter, or to begin a new one.

Used as a beginning of a new chapter, or section, depending on how your story is divided, if a period of a month or so is involved, the Flea Hop can turn into what we might call the Long Jump. The technique is the same. Here's how you might do it:

(Beginning of New Chapter)

"April is the cruelest month. . . ." T. S. Eliot had said that and Ellen who admired him inordinately and who, on occasion, wrote poetry herself, felt she could not have expressed it better. Every day of the entire cruel month, Joel had passed her in the hall without speaking. She had gotten a C-minus in a chemistry test that was almost certain to foul up her grade average for the semester and keep her out of the Honor Society. And at home, it seemed she could do nothing right. Greta continued to act the part of the wicked stepmother. As for her father, he was so completely under Greta's spell that he took her side on everything. And then, miraculously on the very day that April changed to May, the world became sunny again. Joel came into the library where she was studying and sat down beside her and gave her his lopsided grin. "Remember me?" he said.

The above transition must be long because it mentions a number of things necessary for the reader to know, but that would be inordinately dull if each event were described in detail.

Sometimes Flea Hops are so easily accomplished they are scarcely noticed, yet still serve their purpose. In the following from *Angel Baker, Thief* (Eyerly), the time lapse could be several days or several weeks. The time is indefinite because there is no need to define it.

> *With the first semester* beginning to wind to a close, everyone was busy with term papers and studying for final exams.

or

> *For days,* Angela helped Mrs. Gardiner with the preparations for Christmas.

A chapter ending with a built-in transition might consist of only six words: *"And so the week went by."*

Look at the way Anthony Trollope handled an apparently long and dull period of time in a single paragraph:

> When Mr. Harding met his daughter at breakfast the *next morning* there was no further discussion on the matter, nor was the subject mentioned between them for *some days. Soon after* the party Mrs. Bold called the hospital, but there were various persons in the drawing room at the time, and she therefore said nothing about her brother. *On the day following* John Bold met Miss Harding. . . .

Another master of transitions is Evelyn Waugh. Glancing at random through the pages of *A Handful of Dust,* you will find:

> *During the early days* of his convalescence . . . Tony lay in the hammock staring up at the thatched roof and thinking about Brenda.
> *Two weeks passed;* there was no sign of rescue but Tony endured the day. . . .
> *Weeks passed endlessly.* . . .
> In *four days* Tony and Dr. Messinger paddled down stream.
> They had finished *Bleak House* and were nearing the end of *Dombey and Son* when the rain came.

You will notice that in the examples given so far, we have been dealing with simple progressions of time. Though some are long, some short, and some indefinite, all are designed in the main to move the story ahead over periods when nothing interesting or important happens.

Sometimes, however, the story must not only move forward in time but "put down" in a different place, one which will involve a new scene or setting. Because the authorial impulse to travel with one's character from here to there—wherever here or there might be—is so strong, true grit is required in such situations. Remember that a straight line in writing as well as mathematics is the shortest distance between two points. Dullsville is apt to lie in between.

Here's how you might go about taking your heroine—she's just turned eighteen and graduated from high school—from her home somewhere in the Midwest to a summer job in New York City, where she will be an intern on a teen magazine.

> Not until all the goodbyes had been said three times over, her suitcases stowed in the back end of the station wagon for the trip to the airport in Des Moines, and she'd been to the bathroom for one last time, did Megan look tearfully at her family arranged around the room and say, "I've changed my mind. I'm not going to go."

The end of the chapter.
Now the beginning of the new chapter:

> High from her room on the twenty-fifth floor of the Barchester Hotel, Megan looked out across the lights twinkling in Central Park. . . . The tiny cars moving along single file on the avenue far below didn't look much larger than the miniature automobiles her brother Tommy collected.

The simple act of saying that Megan is in a hotel room in New York, *places* her there. It would have been just as simple, and possible even better, to have had the chapter begin with Megan standing on Fifth Avenue, butterflies in her stomach, staring up at the huge building housing the offices of the magazine she has come to work for.

In either version, you as well as your reader have escaped a boring ride to the airport with her father, who, worried about the farm, is mostly silent, a long layover in Chicago, a delayed takeoff, and an uneventful flight to New York where the action of the story is about to begin.

The same kind of short cut can be taken in changing a scene from the living room to the bedroom, from bedroom to garden, or from school to tennis court. There's no need for you to go along unless something is going to happen.

BACK IN A FLASH

The Flashback, like the Flea Hop and the Long Jump, is another means of switching time and place, but instead of enabling readers to leap forward or over inconsequential events, the Flashback gives readers an important glimpse into the past without burdening them with a series of events that have nothing to do with your story.

Although a flashback can occur anywhere in your novel, its only purpose should be to inform the reader of something he needs to know. It can be trivial, or it can be of vital importance.

If well done, a flashback can transport a reader from the present to the past and then back to the present so easily he scarcely knows he has made the trip.

Another similarity between transitional devices and the flashback is the ease with which it can be accomplished. You needn't even roll off a few extra spaces on your typewriter.

Almost anything can trigger memory and serve as a reentry to past experience. For all of us, sense impressions—a snatch of song, the aroma of home-made bread, the taste of cotton candy, even the sight of a pair of dirty running shoes in the back of a closet—may evoke an earlier time, a remembered event. This experience is such a common phenomenon in all our lives that it seems perfectly normal, not manipulative when we run across it in fiction. So much of our mental world depends upon association that the technique is less a device of fiction than an aspect of reality.

Once the flashback scene is over, all you have to do is provide the landing gear to bring your reader firmly back to the present.

The following examples will show you how easy it is to take off and return.

Angela, in *Angel Baker, Thief* (Eyerly) is eleven years old when she receives an invitation to a birthday party given by the prettiest and most popular girl in her sixth grade class. In the following flashback, the invitation is the magic key that takes Angela back to the age of five. It gives the reader much important information about Angela's family, then returns her to the age of eleven again. Here, it is the *birthday party* that anchors the scene:

> Angela had no sooner read the *invitation* than she began to worry. Birthday parties meant presents. She knew that, though she hadn't had a party herself since she was five, before her father lost his good job in Little Rock. In fact, she hadn't even seen her father since he left to look for work in what he called the "oil fields" and that had been six months before. Always, for a time after he left home, he'd write. And when he did her mother was always cheerful.
>
> "We heard from Daddy," she'd say, the minute Angela got home. Sometimes it was a letter propped up on the kitchen table between the salt and pepper and a big jar of Jif, but more often it was a postcard showing some point he'd passed through. Perhaps it would be profiles of the Presidents Washington, Jefferson, Lincoln, and Theodore Roosevelt carved on those mountains in the Black Hills, or a picture of Pikes Peak, or the Mormon Temple in Salt Lake City. She'd learned quite a lot of geography from those postcards.
>
> If her mother was especially cheerful, she knew her father had found work, and sent money as well. Most of the time, however, the only message was, "No work here. Moving on. I love you all. Daddy."
>
> At the time of Kathy LeGraff's birthday party it had been months since even as much as a postcard had arrived at 2020 Gower Street.

The following flashback begins in a high school study hall. The reminder—the clicking of the clock—moves the story backward in time to tell the reader something of great importance that happened the year before. It is the teacher's voice that moves the

WRITING YOUNG ADULT NOVELS

story back to the study hall again:

> Because Mrs. Hayden was a tyrant, study hall where the seniors were taking another one of their tests was so quiet you could hear the sound of the pages in the blue books being turned. But at the moment, Joanna wasn't taking the test. She was remembering. It was the clicking of the clock on the wall—if the room hadn't been so silent she couldn't have heard it—that sent her mind racing back to the waiting room of the abortion clinic. There had been a clock on the wall there, too, clicking away the minutes until her turn would come.
>
> "Joanna!" At the sound of her name, her heart thumping, she snapped to attention.
>
> But it wasn't the clinic nurse who called her. It was Mrs. Hayden. "If you aren't able to finish the test, Joanna, you may as well hand in your paper. Certainly there's no use sitting there and crying about it."

A careful reading of Ernest Hemingway's short story "Fathers and Sons" will show how a master goes about it: The story begins with the father, Nick Adams, traveling by car from here to there—he does not say where, except that it is somewhere in the South—with his young son asleep on the front seat beside him. The countryside, with its clearings where the cotton has already been picked, and its thickets, its fields that still have corn, soy beans and peas in them, looks to Nick like quail country, the kind of country where his own father had taught him to hunt as a boy.

It is the simple act of thinking about his father that leads us back into Nick's boyhood and keeps us there until a small voice says, "What was it like, Papa, when you were a little boy and used to hunt with the Indians?" Nick, who had not known the boy was even awake, is startled. It is a neat touch that at this very juncture, it is the Ojibway Indians with whom he has grown up in Northern Michigan about whom he is thinking. From this point on until the end of the story, we are once more back in the present, back in the car, driving from here to there, somewhere in the South. It is an added bonus that these final two and a half or three pages consist almost entirely of conversation between Nick and his small son, creating dialogue that is just about as perfect as it is possible to write.

130

Flashbacks, however, like any good fictional device, can be misused or overused. Spaced too closely together they can confuse readers to the point that they do not know whether the action being described took place in the past or is once more taking place in the present. Rather than allowing this to happen, consider merging several flashbacks into one. Sometimes you can come up with a different and shorter way of dealing with that bit of past history that you must get into your story.

For instance, instead of having a full-fledged flashback that takes a character back to the summer she was fourteen and given her first kiss by a boy named Dave, who will probably play no part in the rest of the story, a mere summary will serve the same purpose. You might do it like this:

> The summer Jenny was fourteen and worked at the local Dairy Queen, she had been kissed by a boy named Dave. Though she hadn't seen him since, it did seem strange she should think of him as she was being kissed by Tony, five years older and considerably more experienced.

Another way to manage the problem of time might be called Backing and Forthing. Doris Faber in *Love and Rivalry* uses it in this manner:

> During the next several years. . . . (forward)
> About three months before she turned nineteen. . . . (backward)
> Some years earlier, for instance. . . . (backward)
> When Charlotte's school finally opened. . . . (forward)

Look for transitional phrases in everything you read. Jot them down. With a little transposition and a little practice you can adapt them to your own use.

Another means of handling time is through the diary or journal in which the date precedes each entry. This tells the reader that nothing interesting happened in the intervening interval or that if it did the diarist will refer to it in the current entry. Books comprised of letters and journal entries, however, are usually regarded as lazy writing, and beginning writers who are often inclined to insert a letter rather than a scene, should beware of them. Letters that readers, as well as editors, *really* like best are ones addressed to them alone.

Gillian Cross uses time to great advantage in her book, *On the Edge.* The story of a kidnapping, it consists of ten chapters, each covering ten consecutive days in August. Not only are chapters so headed, they are broken down into specific hours during each of the twenty-four when certain exciting events take place, all of which add immediacy to the writing and make the book hard to put down.

In *See Dave Run* (Eyerly) the story of a fifteen-year-old runaway boy is told by twenty-three different narrators. After Joe Rettig, Dave's best friend, tells us that Dave has finally carried out his threat and split, time grimly marches on as each of the narrators, in turn, tells of his encounter with Dave at different points during his long and fruitless search for his father.

Although all the devices mentioned will not fit all situations, they are basically the same for all fiction. Once you have mastered them, they are yours forever. And, always, the better the writer the more skillfully the passage of time is handled.

The passing of time itself has so fascinated some authors that they have built a *magnum opus* around it: notably, Marcel Proust, one of the most famous literary figures of his generation, whose *Remembrance of Things Past* required seven volumes. Anthony Powell, a distinguished British author, achieved literary fame with his *Dance to the Music of Time*, which required a dozen.

Although you, at this point, are only writing *one* book, it is wise to be on the lookout for transitions, flashbacks, and timely devices in everything you read. Soon you will find that they leap right off the page and you have unconsciously absorbed new ways of handling time from reading adult novels as well as those written for the adolescent.

eleven

ALL'S WELL THAT ENDS WELL

———◆———

"A whole is that which has a beginning, a middle, and end," wrote Aristotle in his *Poetics*. He went on to explain that "a well constructed plot, therefore, must neither begin nor end at haphazard. . . ." If good beginnings are important, good endings are a must and often are just as hard to achieve. Certainly writing "The End" on the last page of your manuscript is not going to do it. Actually, the key word here is *achieve*. You can only properly write "The End" when you have achieved the goal toward which you have been laboring these many long months. The ending is the reason for writing your book in the first place. It is what you owe your reader for choosing your book from among the many on the shelves of the library or book store.

So far you should have an interest-grabbing beginning and a middle which carries the reader from crisis to mounting crisis with developing intensity. We can graph your progress in this manner:

  Climax

                                  Complication

                        Complication

              Complication

         Conflict

    Introductory
      Situation

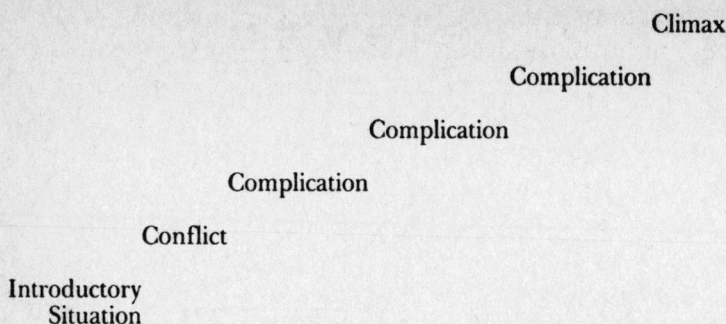

Now that you have reached the climax or turning point, the end is in sight.

Some way you must now bring the reader down from this high point by resolving the initial conflict and its various complications in a manner satisfactory to all concerned: characters, readers, and you the author. We may term this movement from now on as the falling action. This winding down or untying (dénouement) begins after the climax and ends with a final resolution:

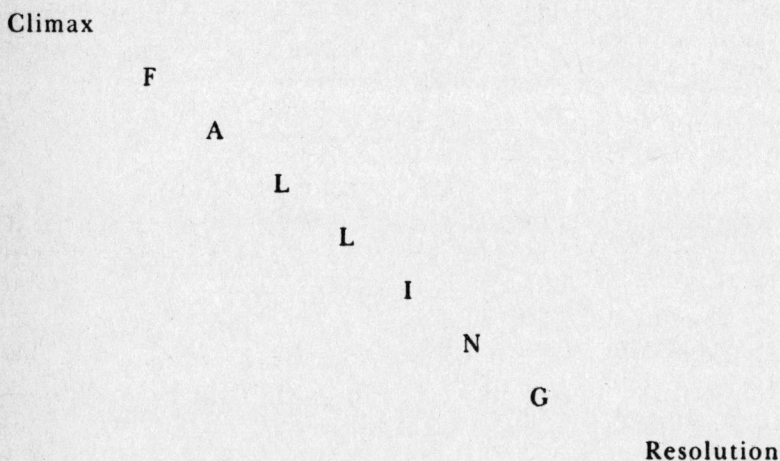

Climax

        F

          A

            L

              L

                I

                  N

                    G

                          Resolution

Endings answer questions posed by the beginning of your story and resolve the conflicts and added complications that provide the framework of your plot line. In other words, endings consist of the untying of the knots that were formed as the conflicts and complications piled up. This final resolution must not be an accident, but must be arrived at step by step, but certainly not as deliberately as the rising action of the middle part of your story. It is more like a wind-up toy. It may take several good turns to wind up the toy, but only a scant second or so for it to unwind. Or you may visualize your plot structure as the waves rolling in from the ocean. Each wave grows in intensity until finally one rolls in so large it breaks with a roar over the sand. The conclusion to your story must roll in with all the force, intensity, and speed of that big wave.

If endings are not to appear "haphazard," it is a good idea for authors to have a fairly good idea of the climax and resolution of their story from the very beginning. Edith Wharton expressed it this way: "I have never understood the mental state of the novelist who starts out without knowing where or how he will end. To me the last page is always latent in the first, but the intervening windings of the way become clear only as I write."

Good endings are the result of a character's actions, working through and creating a plot pattern. The resolution of your story may not be the solution for your teenage reader facing a similar problem, but it must be the logical solution for your protagonist because of what that character is and what has happened in the course of the story.

HAPPY OR SAD ENDINGS

When young readers were polled about the kind of endings they liked, the answer usually lay somewhere between positive and satisfactory. While they say a too happy ending is not true to life, neither do they want the book they have enjoyed reading to end on a note of doom and gloom. The test of a really good ending, one young teen told us, is "when you get to the end of the story and you know it's over, but you still turn over those one or two blank pages at the end to see if there is more. That particular book has been so good you just don't want it to end."

Although we are accustomed to think of books as having only two kinds of endings—happy or sad—there is a large middle ground. For the sake of discussion, and these divisions are arbitrary, we can point out the various choices an author has in ending a story.

Happy Ever After is the typical fairy tale ending, upbeat and optimistic. Such endings are the trade mark of light love romances, adventure tales, romanticized historical novels and some problem novels. Such stories allow all of us to live for a time in an imagined world where good is rewarded, evil punished, and hope springs eternal. Some examples of this type of resolution include *The Divorce Express* (Paula Danziger), *From the Mixed-up Files of Mrs. Basil E. Frankweiler* (E.L. Konigsburg), *If Winter Comes* (Lynn Hall), the happy ending in the latter only within the confines of the book, since the threat of nuclear war remains with us in the world beyond fiction.

Positive and Hopeful is a more realistic conclusion, more true-to-life although it still leaves the teenage reader feeling upbeat that things in the future are not going to be quite so difficult as the troubles the protagonist has experienced in the story. Most Young Adult literature probably falls in this category of conclusions, since most writers for teenagers have faith in the future and in the younger generation. Such endings occur in *Where The Lilies Bloom* (Vera and Bill Cleaver), *Dinky Hocker Shoots Smack* (M.E. Kerr), *Tiger Eyes* (Judy Blume).

Satisfactory endings, to a young reader, are "the way it really is" or as one teenager said, "The author didn't make everything work out perfect." A 1985 novel by Hila Colman, *Weekend Sisters,* evoked this comment. Most modern problem novels for adolescents make use of this contemporary realistic conclusion. Other books of this type are *Home Before Dark* (Sue Ellen Bridgers), *The Outsiders* (S.E. Hinton), *A Separate Peace* (John Knowles).

Sad and Downbeat endings are not necessarily to be avoided by authors of teenage novels. Stories that deal with death, loss, failure, suicide, and such impel the young reader to spend some time thinking about the impact of the story after the reading is finished. Such endings are often useful in illustrating, but not stating, a theme, moral, or lesson that the author wishes to implant in the young reader's mind. Such stories have the elements of tragic in them and the resolution can provide a catharsis for the young readers by relieving fears, guilt, or pity through the emotional identification with the tragic event. Sadness enhances joy. Authors who have made use of this kind of resolution include Paul Zindel in *The Pigman,* Scott O'Dell in *Island of the Blue Dolphins,* Katherine Paterson in *Bridge to Terabithia.*

Negative If Not Hopeless conclusions can have an extremely jarring effect on a young reader, and if this is the desired effect, this type of ending is useful to illustrate graphically the effect of some drastic choices (suicide, drugs). Some successful books employing this type of conclusion include *The Chocolate War* (Robert Cormier), *Are You In The House Alone?* (Richard Peck), *Go Ask Alice* (Anonymous), *See Dave Run* (Eyerly).

TYING UP THE LOOSE ENDS

With your chosen ending in mind, you must now devise the steps that will lead your reader toward the desired conclusion. This will entail the practical consideration of tying up or snipping off all the dangling threads you have introduced along the way to complicate the plot.

In teenage novels it is advisable to pull everything together and round out the events in as unobtrusive a manner as possible so that a reader's only awareness of what you have done is complete satisfaction. Certainly as you move toward your final resolution, you will rely heavily on scene rather than summary, on character dialogue rather than author exposition or explaining. Let your protagonist do the discovering, the wrapping up, the unraveling in actual scenes where the reader can share each event. Keep your young readers in mind as you devise these scenes of falling action. Leave something to their imaginations. Suggest rather than explain in detail. Show rather than tell.

Read Ibsen's drama *The Doll House* and see how he shows that Nora is definitely leaving her domineering husband. The playgoer or reader wonders if she is leaving him for good. Ibsen answers through a stage direction for Nora. She slams the door! Often the final resolution can be carried out in a mere sentence or even in one word, but only if the author has led the reader step by step, scene by scene, down to the desired resolution. How many steps downward should the action fall? The number depends upon how many loose ends are to be resolved. Certainly an author should avoid rambling on past the point where the main conflict has already been resolved.

On her second book, Eyerly had labored for almost a week on what she believed to be the final chapter. She explained her plight to a friend, a successful fiction writer. "Are you sure you're not through and don't know it?" she asked. The friend was right. Eyerly scrapped the week's work, added a new paragraph to a previous chapter, and wrote "The End." Yes, finishing off your story with just the right flourish can be just as tricky as attempting to end a social conversation gracefully. Take heart. Hadley Irwin wrote thirteen different versions for the ending of their first published novel.

VARIATIONS FOR ENDINGS

Sometimes experienced authors, rather than dragging a story out beyond its actual ending, will resort to a short epilogue or afterword. This device, if used artfully, can work, but if it appears to be just an easy way out, resist the temptation.

The advantage of the epilogue is that one can jump forward in time and show the effect the conflict and complications of the story can have on a now-older protagonist. Some teenage readers need this type of projection into the future. To a teenager, tomorrow is nonexistent. The heartaches and fears of today are all they can see. At sixteen, it is difficult to realize that things will eventually get better. The epilogue ending verifies for young readers that there is a future awaiting them.

One eighth grader asked an author why she ended a book a certain way. Sensing that the young reader was not satisfied with the conclusion, the author reassessed the resolution. The ending of the story rounded off and solved the problems contained in the novel, but it did not project the future of the boy-girl relationship. Sometimes teenagers need the assurance that there is a future for them in this nuclear age. In such cases, an afterword or epilogue might enhance your resolution.

The surprise ending or the sudden reversal conclusion has been used frequently in short stories, murder mysteries, or adventure novels. The resolution in mysteries is often done in one

fell swoop where the detective from Scotland Yard assembles all
the suspects into the drawing room and in one long expository
sequence explains how he solved the crime. Such surprise endings can be useful if the author is completely fair with the reader
in preparing for the reversal and that the outcome is revealed in
a perfectly natural and logical manner.

This type of conclusion should not be used just for shock
benefit, but if used for a definite purpose, it can be effective.
Care must be taken, however, that the reversal or surprise is not
based on mere chance or coincidence. This results in plot manipulation, and such coincidental resolutions are readily spotted by
perceptive young readers. A good rule to keep in mind is that
the nearer you are to the ending of your story the less you will
want to depend on coincidence or chance.

A teenage novel may have an indeterminate or open ending where the main conflict of the plot is not completely solved at
the conclusion of the story. One of the best endings of this type
belongs to Nat Hentoff's *Jazz Country*. We rate it highly because
1) although Tom Curtis has made his decision to go to college
(the right one, most readers will believe), 2) he has not locked the
door on leaving college for a year to play in a jazz band, 3) and
beyond that, the reader sees that Tom has an even broader and
important future with the opportunity to effect sociological
change between blacks and whites. This is how Hentoff does it:

> I'm still not absolutely sure I'm going to stay here at
> Amherst. I may quit any time and try to get a gig playing back
> home. But I'll probably stay at least until the end of the next year.
> There's a guy who teaches sociology who really cooks, and I can
> take his course next year. He's very strong on getting people in
> neighborhoods like Danny's to organize themselves to change
> things. I still remember that cop in the cellar and I wonder what
> the sociology cat has to say about changing that scene. But, much
> as I'm looking forward to his course, there are nights when I'd
> give anything to be in that Volkswagen with Godfrey. After all, I
> could take one year off somewhere along the line. Couldn't I?

You will notice that Hentoff has accomplished in this ending
something we have not mentioned before. In the last two words,
he has involved the reader in the final decision.

AN OBJECT THAT MEANS

With the telling of your story and the illustrating of your theme through the character's actions, you will see as you draw toward your conclusion that some patterns or recurring images are emerging. The conclusion of your novel is a fine place to reemphasize your theme, unobtrusively, and to covertly employ an image or object that now has come to be a meaning-bearing device. For instance, in Judy Blume's *Tiger Eyes*, the sack of clothes that is kept hidden in the closet becomes symbolic of the way Tiger Eyes is able to distance herself from her father's death. In other words, a small, apparently insignificant thing has come to mean a much larger thing or, to be more exact, the concrete object has come to symbolize an abstract truth.

To illustrate further, in *The Lilith Summer,* twelve-year-old Ellen agrees to "lady sit" with seventy-seven-year-old Lilith to obtain money to buy a ten-speed Raleigh bicycle. Lilith, on the other hand, agrees to baby sit with Ellen to get money to buy new aluminum screens for her back porch. At the end of the story, when Ellen rides up on her new bicycle and Lilith is standing inside her newly screened porch, the reader realizes that the bicycle and the screens now carry a meaning of their own: the love that has grown between the young girl and the older woman and the need the old and the young have for each other. Likewise the bicycle and the screens illuminate or reemphasize the basic theme of the book as expressed by Lilith: "We may be coming from opposite sides, but we should be able to see eye to eye."

Authors should use symbolism with care, for images that mean are not mere decorative baubles to drop into a story for show. Objects that come to mean must grow naturally and organically from the story's setting, characters, and plot. Not that your young readers will recognize the import of the images, but the use of such symbolism can add a depth and richness to your story.

FINALLY

A good ending must be a natural, logical outgrowth of a story's action. It is no place to play tricks on your reader. Your final paragraphs should contain your best writing: clear, brief, to the point. Here is a last chance to demonstrate your theme. You will be tempted to tell rather than show, but resist. Keep yourself, as an author, out of the picture and be sure not to preach or moralize. Your ending should be the icing on the cake.

Knowing where to stop can sometimes pose as difficult a problem as deciding where to begin. All of us, at one time or another, have read books where the story actually ended two or three chapters before the author decided to end it. If you have written a story with a well-constructed plot, peopled by believable characters who are motivated by the cause and effect of events, your ending should pose no problem. Think back to your initial theme. What about life did you want to reveal to the young reader? Will the reader have discovered this awareness or understanding from the events of the story? Do the beginning, middle and end make up a unified whole?

TENSE, TONE, VOICE, AND MOOD

———————◆———————

You can play a musical instrument by note, learning the names of key signatures and all the rest of the musical nomenclature, or you can play an instrument by ear, if you are blessed with perfect or near perfect pitch. The same is true of writing. You can become an expert grammarian and understand the workings of gerunds, participles, and such, or you can be so fluent in the nuances of your mother tongue that you see no need for the grammar or "science" of the language.

It is interesting to note that for many years early American educators saw little benefit in teaching a course in one's own native tongue. Instead students studied Latin and Greek, and it was not until the middle of the nineteenth century that educators deemed it necessary to include a course in English grammar, which, ironically, was based on Latin grammar. Certainly, though, a basic knowledge of grammatical terms and how they affect clear expression can be an aid in writing effectively. Sadly, however, the reverse is not necessarily true; the errorless grammarian does not always make an effective writer. However, it will not harm a beginning writer of Young Adult literature to be aware of tense, tone, voice, and mood.

A TENSE SITUATION

Time relations are indicated by the tenses of verbs, and we usually use these tenses without thinking. Perhaps it is not necessary to know that these verbs are grouped together in a system of six tenses: present, past, future, present perfect, past perfect, future perfect. It is important, however, to be aware of the six tenses when you tell your story even if you don't know the grammatical name for what you are doing.

In relaying news, describing an event, or writing to a friend, the past tense is the most natural. We simply tell what has happened, and in the telling, the story becomes real, part of a record. It *happened*.

An author friend of ours tells of a young reader who was upset because of a certain turn of events in one of the friend's books. "I didn't want Barry to come back."

"But Mary Lou, he did," our friend said. "He did come back."

"I was afraid so," said the girl and turned away. The story had been very real to her. The oafish Barry was back, and that was that.

Because of this sense of reality, the past tense has been the traditional one for authors to use and is rightly called "the author's most precious tool." *Past tense indicates something that took place in the past and ended in the past.* Correlating with *past* tense is the *past perfect*, which denotes an event that had already happened when other events in the past occurred. Past perfect can become a quagmire full of "had's" if a writer is not careful. For instance, you are moving along with your story in past tense and you want to relate an incident that happened four years before the action of your story and so you begin: "Four years before, Alan *had* met this same girl at a beach party he *had* attended when *he had* been visiting his cousin Jeff in California."

If you continue in this deadly past perfect, you will have a proliferation of "had's" dotting your manuscript. The solution is to establish the past perfect in one *"had-phrase"* and quickly move to past tense. The first "had" will signal your reader the slip back in time: "Four years before, Alan had met this same girl at a beach party. He was visiting his cousin Jeff in California." Now

144

you can move from summary to an actual scene from four years ago, keeping the scene in plain past tense.

Paradoxically, if you are writing a science fiction story that takes place in the year 2800, you can establish the time and write in the usual past tense. To employ the future tense for such a story, of course, would be completely impossible.

In recent years, perhaps for the sense of immediacy it creates, the present tense has been used more frequently. Part of Paula Danzinger's appeal in *The Cat Ate My Gymsuit* is the use of this simple present which creates the illusion for the reader that the story is actually happening *now*. *The Free Zone Starts Here* by prize-winning English author John Wain is another example of excellent present-tense storytelling and fits well with the eerie subject. The seventeen-year-old narrator is able to communicate with his younger sister who was killed in a plane crash. This ability leads to a new understanding of his sister and the healing of a breach between him and his parents.

You will find, however, that although you are using present tense in your story, it is extremely easy to drop back into past tense without intending to do so, especially when it comes to a scene and the use of attributives. The "he said's" now must become, "he says." Listen to a modern teenager tell about an exciting event that happened: "And then he goes, 'What do you mean?' And I go, 'Just what I said.' " Writers in striving for the reality of the moment may be copying today's teenage jargon.

An axiom states, "Don't change horses in the middle of a stream." For the beginning writer for young adults, a corollary could be, "Don't change tenses in the middle of a theme." For a first novel, stay with the past tense and be consistent throughout your story. Of course Charles Dickens slipped into present tense for a few chapters in *Bleak House* as did Faulkner upon occasion, but again the old rule holds: if you understand the rules, then you can break them, if it works for your story and does not distract your reader.

Shifts in tense must be clearly indicated to the reader and plainly motivated by the action or the qualities of the character. Unmotivated shifts confuse young readers. Tell your story as if it is happening now or tell your story as if it had happened. Erratic tense shifts take such forms as:

1. Past to present: "I got off the plane and looked around. There is Mother and behind her, my father." (Change *is* to *was*.)
2. Two events happened at different times: "When I forgot my speech, I was so upset because I practiced saying it over fifty times." (Change to *had* practiced.)
3. Shift from direct to indirect quotation: "He said there will be a new school built within the year." (Change to *would* be.)

Not that shifts in tense do not work effectively when properly used. Perhaps in none has it been more effective than in *I Am the Cheese* by Robert Cormier, which since its publication in 1977 has won a place for itself among superior novels for young adults. It is a two-fold, first-person story of a journey. On one level it tells of a young boy's search for his father, and on another level, it is the story of a desperate journey through the mysteries of his troubled mind. Intricately structured and highly effective, the novel uses the present tense when Adam is traveling the interstate on his bicycle looking for his father. It switches to the past tense following insertion into the narrative of taped recordings of Adam's interviews with a psychiatrist who is trying to unlock the secrets of the past.

In *Someone to Love Me* (Eyerly), the story of fifteen-year-old Patrice who becomes pregnant and keeps her baby, the author midway in the book switches abruptly from past tense to present. This chapter, which has no numerical heading as do all the other chapters, is titled "The Long Hot Summer" and allows the reader to cover quickly a three-month period, yet at the same time conveys the endlessness of Patrice's days during the fourth, fifth, and sixth months of her pregnancy. When she enters a school for pregnant teenagers in the fall, the story switches back to the past tense.

Perhaps because they are dealing with a problem that has not been solved, black authors of Young Adult books often find the present tense particularly suited to describing the experience of growing up black in America. Bernie MacKinnon uses it well in *The Meantime*. Beginning when a rock is thrown through the window of the suburban house into which young Luke has recently moved with his family, it tells the story of his struggle to survive in the new suburban high school that soon turns into a war zone where white kids challenge black kids, and beatings and retaliations are an everyday occurrence.

It is equally effective in Ernest J. Hines's *A Long Day in November,* a story of life in the rural black South of the 1940s. However, switching tenses is difficult at best. Overdoing it can be disastrous.

To determine what tense you should use for your novel, try each out for a dozen pages or so. Sometimes it may be necessary for you to move back and forth a half a dozen times or more before discovering what works best. Although there are some gains in using the present tense, there will also be some losses. As you write, you will find out what they are.

TONE

Tone is a subtle revelation of an author's attitude toward the writing and suggests the overall stance of the writer. Tone, then, is the impression the reader receives of the author's attitude toward the subject. Tone can be ironic, humorous, nostalgic, serious, frivolous, formal, happy, condescending, intimate, academic, compassionate, loving, critical.

Tone can be completely unintentional on the part of the author or it can be a carefully planned technique. Certainly an ironic approach to a story would be a decision an author would plan, and, incidentally, an attitude that is not always successful with a young adult reader. Young readers tend to take what is printed on the page as truth and not to comprehend the tongue-in-cheek attitude of the ironic stance of the author.

Tone is readily conveyed by the author's choice of words or diction. If the tone is one of displeasure, words that connote boredom or frustration or anger carry this attitude: the musty smell of a house, the stark picture of a wolf posed on a snow-swept hill, the monotonous ticking of a kitchen clock.

Sentence structure can also convey tone. Short, terse sentences can convey anger, fear, frustration. Longer, more complex sentences can carry a feeling of expectation or suspense. Passive voice can depict a situation where the subject of the sentence is deprived of its power to act and must be acted upon.

An author's selection of images or image patterns in a story can easily indicate the values and attitudes imprinted on the story, probably even more so than actual events within the story. A bicycle for Ellen and aluminum screens for Lilith in *The Lilith Summer* (Hadley Irwin) signify the author's attitude toward the wants and even greed of everyone.

Sensory impressions invariably display a writer's feelings. In attempting to communicate what you as an author feel so that your young reader can feel the same way, you must employ all five senses. Such selection gives tone and fuller meaning to your story. Perhaps tone is better described as *color,* for tone is to the art of writing as color is to the art of painting. Tone is never overt, but always implicit, hidden neatly between the lines of the story.

VOICE

Voice is the question of whether the thrust of an action goes from a subject to an object or whether the subject is acted upon by the object: "John hit the ball" (active voice). "The ball was hit by John." (passive voice). Sometimes, however, passive voice is the only available choice. This occurs when the subject producing the action is unknown: i.e., "The First National Bank was robbed last night." Useful, you can see, because no one knows who robbed the bank.

Passive can be used effectively to slow down the action of a story in order to create suspense or to delay a foreshadowed event, since sentences in passive voice contain more words than those in active voice. Passive is convenient too when the object of an action is deemed more important than the subject instigating the action ("The bank will be closed next week." Whoever will be responsible for the closing of the bank is unimportant) or if you wish to soften a blow ("A mistake has been made" instead of "You messed up") or when the receiver of an action is of greater interest than the giver ("Thousands of soldiers were aided by the Red Cross"). If you wish to convey a certain formality, the passive can be used ("The assignments have been distributed").

An author has the choice of using either active or passive

voice, but passive should be used only for a definite purpose. Weak uses of the passive to be avoided are: 1) shifts in voice from active to passive within the same compound sentence making a cat-and-dog sentence where the first part of the sentence is passive and the second part switches to active (The birthday party was planned by Mother, and Jane issued the invitations), 2) shifts in voice within a short paragraph, which can be most frustrating for a reader with its needless words. Observe the following two passages:

> Mrs. Smith knew what she had to do. The floor had to be scrubbed. The parlor had to be dusted. Then she had to sweep off the front porch.

or

> Mrs. Smith knew what she had to do. She had to scrub the floor and dust the parlor. Then she had to sweep off the front porch.

3) Also avoid a passive construction which does not serve a purpose, such as "The first prize was won by my sister and me."

The use of passive without a purpose can become wordy, lumbering, and often pseudoacademic. In many cases it is the mark of the amateur writer, so use the passive with care and understanding.

Illogical tense sequences, harsh clashes in tone, and overuse as well as misuse of the passive voice are slips that often occur in a first draft, but with careful attention during revising and rewriting, they will become patently obvious to the caring writer upon a second or third reading. Even though your grammar sense may be a bit rusty, take heart. Most such errors are, in reality, errors in plain simple logic.

MOOD

"I'm in the Mood for Love," published in 1935, was one of the favorite songs of that period. Hummable and haunting, it is still heard and enjoyed today. Duke Ellington's "Mood Indigo," published four years earlier, has by now assumed classic status. It is not hard to understand why both are memorable. They are mood songs. Through a combination of words and music, they evoke emotions that would be difficult to express any other way.

Mood plays a similar role in novel writing. Defined, it is the dominant emotional effect produced by an author's selection of descriptive details in creating a scene for an action to take place. It differs from tone in that tone establishes the narrator's stance or attitude toward the material of the story. Mood covertly suggests and enhances the emotional response the author wishes to evoke from the reader. It is a chameleon, taking on the color of its surroundings and can be used anywhere. It can be fleeting, lasting only for a sentence or a paragraph, or it can be sustained throughout an entire chapter.

Principal mood tools are the weather, music, color, the five senses, or any detail of description. Either alone or in combination with others, each is effective in almost any situation and often is used so skillfully that the reader is scarcely aware of just how a certain feeling of happiness, sadness, fear, anticipation, dread, horror, dreaminess, or excitement has come about.

To use music as an example:

> Stephanie had been happy until the boy with the oboe moved into the other half of the duplex. At first, she hadn't even known that the slender black tubular thing he blew into as he sat night after night on his half of the front porch, *was* an oboe. Out of sight, inside her own front door, she sat listening to the mournful strains. Sometimes thin and reedy, other times harsh-sounding, it seemed that the music was crying, tormented, asking for release from that thin black body.
>
> That the music was having a similar effect on others was something Stephanie had not thought about until she saw the neighbors had begun to gather, never coming too close, usually staying on the fringes of their own small front yards, listening. Strangely, she thought of the Pied Piper, who had lured the children of Hamlin to their death.

Contrarily, music can evoke happiness, gaiety, romance, abandon, or even hysteria. Marching bands, old songs, the rhythmic accompaniment of cicadas to other sounds of the night, even the "silent music of the spheres" of which Shakespeare wrote in *Twelfth Night,* can contribute to the mood in which you envelop your story.

Dark days, rain, cloudy skies, wind, wet leaves, naked branches tapping against a dripping window pane, bone-chilling cold—all create mood of a certain kind, just as sunny days, blue skies, gentle breezes, budding leaves, tender blossoms, puffy white clouds create another as do all the variations of summer, harvest to drought.

Colors evoke certain moods, as do smells: coffee perking, bacon frying, steak sizzling on the grill and, in contrast, acrid smell of burned food, the stench of rotting flesh. Some words, in and of themselves, produce mood. *Derelict, stark, haunting, chilly, icy, skeletal* are almost guaranteed to bring on shivers. For words of the opposite effect try *limpid, peaceful, sensual.* The list can go on and on. Even the sound of words can create a mood by mimicking the sounds they describe: *murmuring, gurgling, hissing, whirring, moaning.* Such words carry the mood by their actual sounds. Some poets claim that front vowels (a,e,i) suggest the light, fragile, and small, whereas back vowels, (o,u) the gloomy, dark, and foreboding.

Two points of caution. Be wary of relying too much on adjectives and adverbs to carry the desired mood. When you establish a mood, use it to enhance the character's action, not to display your own virtuosity with words. Overdoing mood can result in purple prose, more commonly known as overwriting.

·thirteen·

REVISING AND REWRITING

◆

You finally type the last paragraph of your novel, and you pull the page from the typewriter and heft your manuscript. You have done it! You have written your first novel and you feel like a surgeon pulling off his mask after a successful operation. Now, for the patient, comes the post-operative care.

Your first draft needs just such tender care and attention. Like the surgeon, who allows the patient to rest before checking back on his health, you might put your manuscript aside and do something entirely different from writing. Play golf. Go on a hike. Even do windows. You will find that your characters keep on living and growing in your mind, but more important, it will give you time to fall out of love with your own words. R & R does not mean Rest and Recreation. It means Rewriting and Revising. Nothing will improve the salability of your novel as much as a cold, calculating reading of your manuscript. Revision demands moral strength, so you will need to clear your mind of all the clutter that goes with the inspiration of creating that first draft and assume the objective role of the critic.

Revision probably goes on all the time: in your mind before you put the words down, as you write, and as you reread what you have written. It is entirely possible to write a first draft that does not need to be touched. If that is true, you probably possess a phenomenal memory or have been writing and revising the rough draft in your head for months. For the rest of us, after the inspiration of creating the first draft is over, we reach a point where our Muse has flown back to Mt. Helicon, and we are forced to go it alone, relying only on our technical sense of plot, character, setting, theme, conflict, rhetoric, and plain old English grammar and usage.

IS THERE A RIGHT WAY?

Revising or polishing is a process as individual as the author. Many prefer making revisions as they go along; others feel compelled to rush on with the story, leaping over gaps and holes and writing until the novel is finished. Sometimes the choice is dictated by the simple circumstance that certain pages have been so worked on that the section becomes unreadable if allowed to cool off. In this case, you will find that the fixing must be done on the spot so that you can proceed apace with your rough draft.

However you choose to deal with revision, you will find it a different process from writing the original. A first draft is often a case of nearsightedness; that is, you are completely caught up with individual sentences, paragraphs, pages, actions of characters, the creation of dialogue, and a balance of scene and summary. Revision gives you the advantage of standing back and looking at the story as a whole. From this perspective, you will be able to see things that you didn't realize were there as well as empty places that need filling in. You will be looking at your manuscript as would an editor or your prospective reader. *You must make yourself come to the manuscript without preconceptions,* no matter how much you may love the characters you have created.

The Critical Read-Through

The first step is to read through your manuscript at one sitting, marking with a large FIX in the margin, sections that you feel are not up to par. This means you must forget you are the author and become the reader. Are your characters consistent throughout? Do they spring from the page as live, human beings? Are their actions and speech consistent with the people you think you have created? Is there a continuity in dates, seasons, and years? Is the setting as clear to the reader as it is to you, the author? Have you included too much background material or have you left too much to the imagination of the reader? Are there long paragraphs or groups of paragraphs that look intimidating on the page because of their length or density? If so, your reader will probably skip over them. In some ways, writing is a visual art as well as an intellectual one. As in newspaper print, white space is important in a novel for the eye to relax and the mind to ponder. When you have finished this first complete read-through, do you face the awful comment, "So what?" or do feel as if you have said goodbye to a good friend?

Interestingly enough, some sections that you have written will astonish you by their effectiveness; however, some parts will cause you to blush at the repetitions and redundancies. Some scholars have criticized Homer for his excessive use of the expression "rosy-fingered dawn," but others have excused the ancient Greek by saying, "Homer nods." Keep a sharp eye out for the parts where you, as a writer, nodded, for it is an absolute rule that if the writer nods, the reader will fall asleep.

Reading your story aloud or taping it can be helpful. This allows you to go back and check on the believability of speech patterns, the flow of sentences, and the rhythm of scene and summary. The ear often picks up what the eye cannot see: awkward sentence construction, repetitive words or phrases, too-long scenes, dialogue in which it is difficult to tell who is speaking, or conversation that is larded with too many "he saids" or "she saids." Be wary, however, of reading your story to friends and relatives for criticism. They have a tendency to be too kind. One competent, objective critic can be of help, but even then, you should rely on your own judgment before adopting anyone's suggestions.

If you have read through your complete manuscript and checked dubious sections, now is the time for rewriting. Some revisions can be accomplished with the aid of pen or pencil; others will demand more creative work at the typewriter. All during this period of your R & R, in addition to the meaning of your words, listen to their cadence or how they go together. Just as some colors clash and some notes of music produce nothing but dissonance, so do some phrases, sentences, and even paragraphs. Proper linkage makes for easier reading. One sentence leads naturally into another. Pages turn faster, and the reader cannot wait to reach the end of the episode.

There is a marvelous scene in Philip Roth's *The Ghost Writer* in which the Great Novelist tells the aspiring young author who has come to sit at his feet and learn, how he spent the morning "moving sentences around." This can be a maddening and time-consuming process. You should prepare yourself for times when changing one sentence, removing a minor character, or even a bit of dialogue will have the same disastrous effect as removing a single card from a house built of cards. The whole structure collapses. Even so do not despair. There are always ways out of such a dilemma. Remember, "We never promised you a rose garden."

The prefix "re" denotes doing it again, whatever the action may be. Revision is looking again. Rewriting is writing again. This need not be an onerous task. You have done the basic work, the rough draft. You have said WHAT you want to say. Now is the opportunity to polish HOW you want to say it. The process can be fun if you enjoy playing with language, searching for the exact word, and shaping sentences into their most effective forms. The original writing requires craft. Revision means re-crafting. With luck and talent and hard work, the result is art.

IN-PROGRESS REVISION

If you must have everything correct before you can proceed, then the process of writing a first draft and revision occur at one sitting. Often the opening paragraph of a story demands this kind of revision. For example, in the writing of one Young Adult novel, it was necessary to introduce the main character, Jesse, to hint that his problem was the typical one of teenagers who feel that their lives are being controlled, to introduce a laboratory analogy which would foreshadow his past behavior which had caused his parents to seek psychiatric help for him and to lay the foundations of Jesse's sensitive and even romantic self, although he displays to the world that of a cynical macho, street-wise kid. Jesse is being sent to his grandfather's farm in the Midwest.

First Attempt

The bus had not made as much as a single turn for the last forty miles. It was as if it were bolted to the pavement and only the highway moved. Fields of dried corn and bean stubble stretched on both sides with an occasional farmstead interrupting the *boring* landscape.

Jesse pressed his face against the window.

"We're 150 miles from the nearest airport. You'll have to catch a bus," his grandfather had said.

As you can see, there is too much author and not enough Jesse. "Boring" is the author's, not Jesse's, telling the reader. The paragraph also lacks the basic metaphor of Jesse's feeling as if he is merely a subject in a laboratory experiment. Logic is dubious too. Jesse could not press his whole face against the window; however, there is a sense of setting implied.

First Rewrite

The bus had passed up every exit for the last forty miles as if it were bolted to a treadmill in some kind of crazy laboratory experiment with movies of scenery moving past on a never-ending screen. Whoever the experimenters were, they had chosen lousy scenery: fields of dry corn stalks and bean stubble with only an occasional farm house or crumbling barn interrupting the emptiness.

Jesse pressed his cheek against the window and heard his grandfather's words again, "We're 150 miles from the nearest airport. You'll have to catch the bus."

The laboratory metaphor is here, but the logic is a bit hazy. The bus actively passes up every exit, yet it is bolted to a treadmill. We do catch a hint of Jesse's voice with the word "lousy." The change of "boring landscape" to "emptiness" is an improvement as is "face" to "cheek." The sense of Jesse's rebellion against the "they's" or the experimenters sets a pattern for further discoveries concerning his past.

Second Rewrite

> The bus had not made a turn for the last forty miles as if it were bolted to a treadmill in some kind of crazy laboratory experiment with movies of scenery moving past on a never-ending screen. And they, the experimenters, had chosen lousy scenery: fields of dry corn stalks and bean stubble went on and on with only an occasional farm house or crumbling barn interrupting the emptiness.
>
> Jesse pressed his cheek against the cold window and heard his grandfather's words again, "We're 150 miles from the nearest airport. You'll have to catch a bus."

This rewrite includes most of the elements the author thought necessary, but the reader must know that Jesse is coming to the Midwest during its ugliest season. The addition of "cold window" prepares the reader that it is March and Jesse is not attending school. The opening sentence is still cumbersome.

Third Rewrite

> Every exit for the last forty miles had flipped by as if the bus were bolted to a treadmill in some kind of crazy laboratory experiment where flashes of scenery moved past on a never-ending screen. Whoever the experimenters were, they had chosen lousy scenery: fields of dry corn stalks and bean stubble with only an occasional farm house or crumbling barn interrupting the emptiness.
>
> Jesse pressed his cheek against the cold window and heard his grandfather's words again, "We're 150 miles from the airport. I can't meet you. You'll have to catch a bus from there."

The initial sentence is now more interesting, and the idea of exits "flipping by" is better than the negative, "the bus not making a turn." The active verb "flip" makes the sentence come alive. Changing Grandfather's words clarifies why Jesse is on a bus when he has come from California.

This process of getting the story started right may seem like spinning your wheels, but it may be done as you are writing the first draft or you may plunge ahead and leave the revision until you have completed the first write-through. Perhaps, when the above story is published, the first paragraph may not resemble any of the above versions. Revision, as you can see, is tinkering, but the rewritten passage must not show the tinkering. The final copy must give the effect of having been written with ease even though you may have spent hours on the one page.

REVISION AFTER THE ROUGH DRAFT IS COMPLETED

Perhaps only perfectionists revise and rewrite as they go along and procrastinators rush through, telling themselves they'll fix it later. The practice does have advantages. As you read through your completed story, you will often realize that patterns and significant images are emerging that you have failed to pick up on, and they could offer interesting hints and foreshadowing for the perceptive reader.

For example in *Kim/Kimi* (Hadley Irwin) Kim, a 16-year-old Japanese American has gone in search of her Japanese father's family. Having been raised in the Midwest by her Caucasian mother and stepfather, she has long felt an innate urge to find out who she really is. She feels American. She looks Japanese. She locates a long-estranged aunt, who accepts her, and a grandmother, who still lives by the strict protocol of Japanese family tradition and will not accept her. The final paragraph in the first draft reads:

> As I wheeled Barbara's old Schwinn slowly down the drive, I looked back. My grandmother, who could not speak English, was standing at the window watching.

In the read-through process, the author discovered that throughout the story, Kim had often studied herself in a mirror, saw herself reflected in the eyes of her peers as being different, and worried about her outside Japaneseness and her inside Americanness. Every teenager faces the inevitable answer to puzzling questions of "Wait until you're older." The story had developed two images, yet they were missing in the concluding paragraph: reflection and waiting. A rewrite was definitely in order. The paragraph was rewritten to read:

> I walked toward the beveled glass door. The lawn dipped down to the street where Barbara's bike stood propped against the curb. I paused, my hand on the door knob. I saw, reflected in the glass, my aunt in her pink shoes, and standing a little behind her, my Japanese grandmother, who could not speak English.
> I did not turn around.
> I would learn to wait. After all, I *was* a Yogushi—half Yogushi, that is.

Call it picking up on loose threads or completing a pattern which consciously or subconsciously had been woven into the narrative, but a second or third or fourth look at your story will almost always reveal something that if changed or added or deleted could enhance the story. However, a competent doctor must know when the patient no longer needs treatment and care. A writer, too, must sense when it is time to stop revising, for caught up in the zeal to rewrite and improve, you may destroy what was effective and good in the first draft. Save the creative impetus you sometimes feel when rewriting for your next novel.

PRUNING

A careful writer will devote one complete read-through to the sole aim of tightening the language by eliminating superfluous words, redundancies, needless repetitions, and author-sounding phrases. Sharpen your pencil to a fine point and prepare to slash a concise path through your overgrown verbiage. Following is a partial list of offending "weeds" that inevitably creep unnoticed into a rough draft:

1. Cut as many articles (a, an, the) as you possibly can.
   "A heavy perfume" to "Heavy perfume"
   "The wind whipped the awnings" to "Wind whipped the awn-

ings."

2. Replace weak verbs trailing a host of modifiers with one vivid verb
   "He went slowly and nonchalantly" to "He sauntered."
   Likewise with nouns and their modifiers. Convert adjectives to verbs
   "Clear, sparkling water" to "Water sparkled."

3. Don't slip into the "there are," "who is," "which are," "it is" mire.
   "There are some people" to "Some people"
   "That party, which was to be my last" to "My last party"

4. Avoid illogical redundancies.
   Change "The reason he was late was because" to "He was late because . . ."
   Change "The fact that he missed the plane" to "Because he missed the plane"

5. Shun the wordy double negative.
   Change "He thought it not unlikely that she would refuse" to "He thought she would refuse."

6. Use the passive voice sparingly.
   "He was accosted by two masked men" to "Two masked men accosted him."

7. Replace, when possible, the static state-of-being verbs (is, are, was, were) with action verbs.
   Change "Father's stories were always exciting" to "Father always told exciting stories."

8. Avoid the repetitious "would" syndrome by using past tense.
   "Often he would escape to the woods" to "Often he escaped to the woods."

9. Watch for meaningless words that creep in: well, just, but, etc.

10. Skirt the inane "hopefully."
    "Hopefully, I can do it" to "I hope I can do it."

11. Don't succumb to the easy cliché.
    "All of a sudden," "quick as a wink," "in one fell swoop," "bolt out of the blue."

You may think you have maimed your manuscript with all the trimming and deletions, but there is an old adage that says that stories are not written, they are rewritten. Gertrude Stein is said to have cut one of Hemingway's paragraphs down to *two* words. Less is more when it comes to writing clear, concise English.

PROOFREADING

Now comes the final inspection. Read your perfected manuscript through, not for plot or setting or character development, but for pure English correctness. Watch for misspelled words, the dirty linen that can brand you an amateur. Place commas correctly, not sprinkled in like salt and pepper. Question marks for questions. Exclamation marks kept at a minimum. Pronoun reference presented clearly. Characters' names spelled consistently throughout the manuscript.

Read your manuscript backwards to spot misspellings, which the eye can miss when caught up in the language, excitement, and suspense that your story offers. It is boring, but it is foolproof.

EDITOR REVISIONS

You may think when your book has been accepted for publication that your work is over, but if you are lucky enough to be assigned a caring editor, you will receive a list of suggested revisions, noted by page number, paragraph, and line. In most cases you will find such suggestions helpful. In some cases, you will see your most prized passages cut to shreds.

It behooves a beginning writer to establish a fine working relationship with the assigned editor, for your editor is as interested as you in producing a product to be proud of and a story that will captivate an audience of young adults. If the suggestion is to rewrite an entire chapter or even an entire section, a writer's first impulse is to fire back a list of justifications; however, it is best to spend a few days cooling down. The situation is similar to a mother's receiving her child's first report card. How could her child appear so stupid? He's smart enough around home.

Approach this final go-through carefully and take your time on making decisions. Re-examine your brain child. Stand off and rethink your writing as objectively as possible. Remember your editor knows what the market will allow, what young readers are demanding, and what librarians, teachers, and critics will accept. If you feel strongly about something, you can argue with your editor, but 99 percent of the time an editor knows best, particularly concerning your first published book. After you have established a reputation as a writer, you can be more vocal about changes in your text.

Publishers and their editors work on a definite schedule, so be prompt and considerate of deadlines for returning your corrected manuscript. Editors do not like "late papers" any better than teachers do. Publishers of Young Adult books usually adhere to a schedule of publishing offerings to appear on a spring list and on a fall list, so you might strive to beat your deadlines.

GALLEY PROOFS

By now you will have lost count of how many times you have read through your story. It is no longer exciting reading for you, but you have one more read-through: the galley proofs. These consist of your book, set up in type and run off on long sheets for your inspection. Now, any changes must be kept to a minimum, for large chunks of rewriting can be expensive for the publishers. One word or one line of text can be altered without too much consternation. At this stage, your words *are* practically engraved in stone.

One author, when a book was in the galley proof stage, discovered that a name given to one of the characters was actually the name of a person living in the community about which the story was written. Luckily, it was possible to make the correction before the book went into final printing, and the author learned a valuable lesson in thorough research.

Perhaps you can see now why another author admitted that she seldom rereads a book she has written. However, it is often invigorating to read one of your own published books a year or two after it has appeared on the market. You will find yourself saying, "Did I write that?"

With careful scrutiny of your manuscript and meticulous self-editing and revising, you will be proud to say, "I *did* write that!"

HIDDEN MESSAGES/ HIDDEN DANGERS

Although the term "raising consciousness" may have become a cliché in the 1980s, the idea behind the concept is important for both writer and reader. Unconsciously, writers convey attitudes, biases, and moral judgments; unconsciously, young readers absorb them. Since Aristotle, the question of whether art is meant to instruct or entertain has been debated. Both are implicit in writing Young Adult novels. No serious writer would wish to deliberately advance negative moral values, perpetuate stereotypes, or compound misjudgments that too often exist in the real world; however, inadvertently, even the most conscientious writer can commit just those errors.

In the long ago, more innocent days of Horatio Alger, Jr., Martha Finley, and Kate Douglas Wiggin, life was portrayed simplistically. Good guys and bad guys were clearly delineated. There was no room for shades of gray. Villains were villains, heroes were heroic, and heroines were pawns of both. Situations were clear. Though evil might triumph for a moment, eventually good won out. No one had ever to puzzle about the amount of evil in good or the amount of good in evil. Old characters were wise or peculiar or senile. Young characters, for the most part, were sweet, naive, malleable except for the occasional and obvious bully, who was so nasty that no one could possibly take him as a role model. And it always was a *him*. Mothers stayed in the kitchen where they obviously belonged. Fathers earned money and knew how to do all the things that their wives were too stupid or too weak to accomplish.

If the story contained characters who were other than white, stereotypes were equally simple. Blacks were lazy, ignorant, good-natured, and had an inborn sense of rhythm. Orientals, whether Chinese or Japanese, spent their time being inscrutable, sly, and devious. Native Americans were either so noble they should have ascended straight to the happy hunting ground or were carting off innocent white children for a fate worse than death.

One can only guess at how many of those characterizations were taken quite seriously by young readers. How much bigotry, distrust, intolerance, and injustice were caused by the hidden messages embedded in such stories? Fortunately, we have become more sensitive to the diversity and the beauty of differences, and less judgmental on the basis of sex, race, age, and life styles. The isms—sexism, racism, agism—are slowly disappearing. Pejorative terms—nigger, kike, Jap, Chink, codger, old maid—are the words of an obvious bigot or dullard. Even the problem of using the pronoun "he" to represent everyone is usually dealt with by simply using the plural. These may seem like small or obvious changes, but they represent, on the surface at least, a raised consciousness.

More dangerous and more insidious are the hidden messages of which even writers themselves are sometimes unaware. No matter how liberated or informed authors believe themselves to be, stereotyped attitudes and values can lurk by implication between the lines.

Sexism

It must be obvious today that sexism extends from stereotypic gender roles to economic responsibilities to parenting patterns. The printed word subtly conveys an author's engrained attitudes and prejudices. Like a hidden voice, these attitudes echo beneath the story. Listen to the echoes in your own work. What are they telling the young reader besides what is explicit on the page? Echoes, you know, resound much longer than a caller's shouts. Hitler knew at least one thing when he ordered the burning of books: books had power.

Most flagrant slips in sexism in a Young Adult novel appear in plotting who does what. Is mother only a mother? Is father an eight-to-five worker? Do only boys have paper routes and mow lawns for extra money? Do only girls baby-sit and wait on tables? Girls and boys have choices today that cross sex boundaries. Mothers are veterinarians, lawyers, judges, dentists, doctors, professors. Fathers are elementary teachers, fashion designers, secretaries, hair dressers. Be careful when you assign roles to your characters that you do not lapse into the old and trite. At best stereotypes make lazy writing. At worst, they are destructive. One author, writing a Young Adult novel, had a young, successful business woman pay a visit to her aunt and slipped nicely into a pit of stereotypes by writing, "She strode into the room, wearing a tailored black suit and carrying, instead of a purse, a leather brief case."

Needless to say, changes were hastily made. Outward appearances should not be a criteria for self-worth. One children's career book of several years back stated that boys can grow up to be pilots; girls to be stewardesses. Boys could be doctors; girls, nurses. That type of overt sexism is past.

Diction, or the choice of words, can betray your values as well as assigning roles to your characters. Girls can be ambitious without being aggressive. Sensitive boys can cry without sacrificing their manhood. Macho is not symbolic of masculinity nor is fickleness of femininity. Words to describe girls that echo sexism can include such expressions as giggling, screeching, trembling, pouting, primping, or shy and weak. For boys such words as these echo the same attitudes: boisterous, rough, cruel, bossy, messy. Sometimes what an author believes speaks so loudly that a young reader will be turned off from the story. After all, the language that you use in your story reflects the way in which you view the world and influences young readers' perceptions of humankind.

Sexism can creep in when you create a family for your character. In an elementary classroom of twenty-five to thirty children, probably no more than five or six will go home after school where a mother is waiting and a father is out providing for the family. Life styles have changed, but even with the change stereotyped generalizations can be found. Not all single-parent families suffer traumatic problems. Not all two-parent homes are happy. Not all latchkey children are lost, depraved, or deprived. Not all children of alcoholics are abused. Not all sex-abused children come from low income families. Behavior often conforms to the stereotypes we use. Perhaps the opposite is more true: behavior creates stereotypes.

Racism

A racist slip is always a sign to the particular ethnic group that the author does not belong to the group or does not understand that culture. Racism tends to classify people of varying shades, arbitrarily, based on myth, ingrained prejudices, learned discrimination and ignorance of historical, genetic, or ethnic facts. As ten-year-old Rap Davis says in *I Be Somebody* (Hadley Irwin), "I know everybody ain't alike, Aunt Spicy, but how come being different makes a difference?" If humankind could answer Rap Davis, there would be no racists in the world. Until that time, authors of Young Adult novels, authors who in reality are shaping the thinking of tomorrow, must be aware that America is made up of a multicultural and multiethnic society. It no longer consists of whites and nonwhites.

Authors take risks when attempting to write from a heritage other than their own, for the stereotypes representing what they think they know about a culture are bound to occur. "Squaw" and "papoose," considered derogatory terms by Native Americans, were terms coined by white men. (Pow-wows and dances are forms of religious expression.) Native Americans do not and seldom did speak in stilted broken-English as did Tonto in "The Lone Ranger." Fences and ownership of land were strange concepts for a people who reverenced and worshipped the earth and nature.

Young Adult literature, in its earlier years, was too often white, middleclass, Anglo-Saxon, Protestant. But that was then. Or was it? Recently a State Superintendent of Public Instruction

in a midwestern state, on giving reasons for his state's high ranking in education said, "Here we're pretty hard-core, middle-
class, white, Protestant, and western European." If educators
are that racially blind, it falls to writers of Young Adult novels to
step beyond their own ethnicity and educate the young of
America in the fascinating racial diversity of their country.

Agism

Respect for elders has been a code of behavior for civilized people even before Moses received the commandment on the stone
tablet. Today, with the senior citizen population increasing, authors might well insist on implanting that respect in young readers' minds. Older people, like everyone else, are individual,
more different than alike. Writers should be careful not to gen-
eralize their characteristics by employing the handy stereotype.
One author was chagrined to find a latent agism neatly tucked
into the text of a Young Adult novel: "Old Mr. Cummings hob-
bled up to the door like a late autumn grasshopper."

A writer can err on the positive side as well. Not all older
people are wise. Not all are tolerant. Not all are sweet and compassionate. They share the same feelings of anger, passion, love,
and hate as any teenager. Grandparents no longer sit in rocking
chairs on the front porch. They play tennis and golf in Florida.
They bicycle in the winter in Arizona. They bask in the sun on
Hawaiian beaches. They drive sports cars and travel in motor
homes. The point is not to play on the infirmities of old age or
use the labels that hint of absent-mindedness and senility, but,
on the other hand, not to romanticize the late years with euphe-
misms such as "golden," "sunset," or "twilight." As with sexism,
so it is with agism: write about individual human beings and pe-
ruse carefully the adjectives and adverbs you attach to their descriptions.

Just as you would not include characters in your story not
necessary to the plot, neither should you omit older characters
because you think they might not appeal to a young readership.
While the average age of the general population has grown older, still many young people have little direct contact with members of the older generation. The traditional family unit, which

at one time consisted of grandparents as well as assorted aunts and uncles, has shrunk. For some young people about the only contact they will have with the past is through television and books.

TO TELL THE TRUTH

In order to avoid covert bias of any kind, you must read with a highly critical eye every reference that might carry a double meaning. Stereotypic statements or characterizations are not difficult to discover, but individual word choice may hide implications the writer does not intend. Note the hidden biases embedded in what seems to be a factual statement.

> The pioneers had to face the *hostile* Indians and a hostile environment. The location of the first homes around the forts was necessary for protection against the Indians. This was an *enemy* that could be faced and conquered. The hostility of the weather was more elusive.

The reasons for revision are clear. Not all Native Americans were hostile, and those who were certainly had adequate reasons when settlers were illegally usurping their land. It is well to remind the reader that the Indians were here first, and whites were the intruders. The fault here is in the connotation of the words. It can easily be revised to read:

> Pioneers had to face the *native* Indians and a hostile environment. The location of the first homes around forts was necessary for protection against the Indians. This was an adversary that could be faced and conquered. The hostility of the weather was more elusive.

A statement regarding Japanese Americans' incarceration during World War II is phrased:

"Hastily built tar paper barracks were the new *homes* for Japanese Americans." Here one word, again because of its connotation, is totally misleading. While thousands did live in these conditions throughout the war, the term "homes" hardly signifies the actual deprivation that occurred.

Even a line as innocuous as "The first blacks who came to America on slave ships . . ." glosses over the truth. The message is hidden in the word "came." While literally factual, it ignores the truth of the way in which they came. They were brought against their will and sold into a life of slavery. In all these cases, the effect, though probably not deliberate, is to excuse the perpetrators of guilt.

It is a matter of remembering who your readers are. They read because they are intrigued by the plot, because they can escape with pleasure to another world created by the author. They know it is fiction—something they do not always comprehend when they view television. The major problem with this audience is that implication, advertently or inadvertently included by the author, is transferred almost by osmosis and subconsciously affects beliefs and attitudes. The moral and intellectual responsibilities an author for young adults must shoulder are staggering.

·fifteen·

YOU'RE ON YOUR WAY

At last the time comes when you type the final period on the last sentence of the last chapter, and YOUR BOOK is finished. You have rethought, replotted, rewritten, refurbished, revised, re-edited, recopied, and you really don't want to read another single sentence of your creation. Now comes the bare bones of getting your novel published.

A published author has merely to send the manuscript off and leave the marketing to an agent. Often a beginning author is not allowed such luxury. While the agent approach can be a vicious circle—to obtain an agent you must have published, and to find a publisher, you need an agent—this is not an absolute. Agents have been known to pick up work they like from a beginning writer. However, there is a way to market your own material.

Before your typewriter has time to cool down, go back to your file and look through the list of markets you have compiled of publishers that might be interested in the type of book you have just completed. Select five or six possible markets, complete with the name of the person in charge of the Young Adult Book department. Check on any changes in personnel in this department. Consult again your *Writer's Market* on what this first publisher on your list wants. The company may want no submissions except through an agent. Cross this one off your list. Another publisher may accept only query letters. Some will accept complete manuscripts for fiction and insist on queries for nonfiction. If the first one on your list wants the former, you may forget about the query letter and bundle up your work and send it off.

THE QUERY LETTER

If the publisher you have chosen insists on queries, you will now face the true test of your writing skill: the query letter. This letter is, in truth, a sales letter. You will be selling the editor on the idea of asking to see your completed manuscript. Envision your editor as a human being sitting at a desk piled high with other query letters and unread manuscripts. Somehow you must, in a letter no longer than one page, grab his attention and make your story sound so intriguing that he can't help but ask to read it in its entirety. As you can see, you will probably find yourself spending more time formulating this letter than you did on a whole series of chapters.

See your query letter in four parts, skillfully woven so that no seams show of PRESENT. PICTURE. PROVE. PUSH.

Present: In your opening paragraph you must present yourself and your story in such a way that the editor's attention and interest is aroused immediately. It should include the title of your manuscript, the central idea or theme, the length, and the publisher's and public's need for just such a book—all this in no more than *three* smooth-flowing sentences that sparkle with originality, but are not necessarily cutesy. The editor should be able to tell after reading your first paragraph whether your book is something that his company might be interested in publishing and investing a considerable amount of money in its production. These two or three sentences will be the hardest paragraph you will ever be required to compose.

Picture and prove: Your second paragraph can be a bit longer and will go into more detail as to why your book is different, how it can meet the reading demands of the young adult market, how your theme is appropriate to the age of the audience and the times, and why you are specifically suited for writing such a book. This paragraph fills in, briefly but in detail, anything further the editor may want to know after his curiosity has been aroused by your opening paragraph.

If one of your characters has stated the theme within the development of the story, this could be a good way to provide the proof. For example, in selling an editor on *The Lilith Summer* (Hadley Irwin), a book which treats the relationship between a twelve-year-old girl and her seventy-seven-year-old baby sitter, the older woman says to the girl when the two are not getting along together, "I'm going off stage and you're coming on. We ought to be able to see eye-to-eye." Such a quote can give an editor more of an idea of the book than a two- or three- paragraph plot summary.

Push: Ask for action in the last paragraph of your letter. Call the editor's attention to any enclosures which you are including and ask specifically for the action you want the editor to take—to request to see your entire manuscript. Be confident in your request. Avoid "If you are interested" or "If you like." An "if" assumes the choice of a negative response. Instead say confidently, "I will send the manuscript at your request."

Short is the key for the query letter. Never should it be more than one page and preferably written in three paragraphs. An ideal model is

Paragraph 1: 3-4 sentences or less
Paragraph 2: 5-6 sentences
Paragraph 3: 1-2 sentences

BUSINESS LETTER FORM

Of course, you will type your letter on good quality paper noncorrasable, 16-lb. bond (with matching envelope) with a clean typewriter and new typewriter ribbon and in proper business form. If you have forgotten the form, check in the library for a text on business letter writing. An efficient and popular form used in today's business world is the block form.

112 Forest Avenue
Des Moines, Iowa 50311

November 3, 1986

Editor Jane Doe
Best Books, Inc.
111 Fifth Avenue
New York City, NY 10017

Dear Editor Doe:

An attention-getting presentation of you as a writer and of your novel goes here in two or three well-thought-out, concise sentences. Do not forget to mention your novel by name, capitalizing the main words of the title and underlining the complete title. Don't use quotation marks for titles of books.

You may single space within each paragraph of your letter and double space between paragraphs. Note that the left margin of your letter is even with no indentations for paragraph. This is the block form, and, as you type, you will see how efficient it is for business letters. Of course, it will be necessary for you to space your letter on the page with as much care as you would mount a picture in a frame. If you have forgotten the proper margins for typing, dig out your old high school typing text. The query letter must make a good first impression on the reader. It is to you the same as the door-to-door salesman's getting his foot in the door.

An editor should be able to read through your query letter in fifteen to twenty seconds. Remember, editors are busy people. With only seconds at hand for you to make a good impression on the reader, you must make your query letter a masterpiece of ingenuity and writing skill.

Sincerely,

Mary B. Writer

Enclosures: synopsis and sample chapters

ENCLOSURES

The information in *Writer's Market* about your publisher may direct you to "query with synopsis and sample chapters." In this case, your query letter should be so fascinating that it will compel the editor to read the enclosed samples of your writing.

For your samples, use the first three chapters or roughly the first fifty pages. Run off ten or twelve copies of each at a professional copy center on good quality paper. With these sample chapters, include a chapter by chapter synopsis of your entire novel. These synopses are mere summaries of the action within each chapter and should not be longer than a three- to four-sentence paragraph.

Place your query letter on top of your sample chapters and synopsis, place unfolded and unstapled in a nine by eleven manila envelope. Include a SASE (Self Addressed Stamped Envelope) for a return answer. To find the proper postage, go to your post office and have them weigh your letter, chapters, and synopsis, and affix the proper FIRST CLASS postage on the SASE. Then place the letter, chapters, synopsis, and the SASE in the manila envelope, and have the postmaster reweigh for the proper outside postage. Check in *Writer's Market* or *Fiction Writer's Market* for the response time to queries and then add two or three weeks to that. Editors are busy, you know. If you have not received an answer to your query letter by that time, use common sense in following up with a letter or a phone call.

PREPARING THE FINAL COPY OF THE MANUSCRIPT

With your query letter off, instead of watching for the mailcarrier, busy yourself with preparing the final copy of the manuscript. If you have access to a word processor, getting a clean copy of your work is no problem. If you can afford a professional typist, your work will be done for you. If you are your own typist, you have your work cut out for you.

Type your final draft on good quality paper with a new typewriter ribbon. In the upper left hand corner of your first page, type your name, address, phone number, and, for convenience, your social security number. If you prefer, this could go in the upper right hand corner, but in any case, be consistent. You will not number the first page, but on each succeeding page, type your name and the number of the page in the upper right hand (easier page turning) corner: Jane Doe—2.

About one-third from the top of the first page, type the title of your book in caps. No need to underline. Space down about four spaces and type the chapter number or title. About two to four spaces down begin the first paragraph of your novel, double spacing each line and indenting five spaces for each new paragraph. Keep a good inch or so margin from the bottom of each page and an inch or so on each side. Begin a new page for each new chapter and remember to number each page. Do not clip or staple your pages.

Keep a dictionary and grammar usage handbook at hand at all times. Your final draft should be error free as far as grammar mechanics are concerned. Misspellings tend to convey an impression of carelessness. Proofread your final copy most carefully. You want your lovely brain child to appear in its most appealing dress.

Purchase two large padded mailers big enough to hold your manuscript and your SASE. Follow the same procedure at the post office as you did in mailing your query. Be sure to include the proper postage for the return of your manuscript. Affix the stamps to the SASE envelope. Do not send money for the return of your manuscript. At all times resist the temptation to do your manuscript up in a fancy binding with gold lettering. Such a practice marks you as a rank amateur.

You may have to wait several weeks for an answer from the publisher, but as soon as you receive a positive response, send your manuscript off with a simple cover letter. This letter, which will follow the same business form as your query, should be but a brief note stating that in response to the editor's request to see your work, you are forwarding the material for their consideration. Address the letter to the editor or assistant editor who answered your query and refer to the date of their answer. Be sure to have a return address on your package and seal your manuscript with stout gummed tape, reinforcing both ends of the envelope. If you do not receive a positive response from the query letter, get out your list of possible publishers and send out another packet of sample chapters and synopsis. Allow three months or longer to hear from a publisher on a completed manuscript. If there is no response after two months, a letter of inquiry is in order or perhaps a telephone call.

MULTIPLE SUBMISSIONS

Sending out more than one query letter at a time or sending your completed manuscript to two or more publishers simultaneously is frowned upon by editors. Sometimes publishers will state that multiple submissions are acceptable, but this occurs only when two publishers are marketing in different fields where they do not come in competition with each other: e.g., religious companies where the same material would appeal to various religious denominations, but the readers of their books would seldom be the same.

Unfortunately, some publishers are not cooperative and keep a manuscript many months only to reject it. This is most unfair to the author.

PERSEVERANCE AND PATIENCE

If the key words for the query letter are *present, picture, prove,* and *push,* the magic words for getting your novel published are *perseverance* and *patience.* If your manuscript is returned to you unaccepted, don't give up. Send it out again and again and again. If it is good and you know it is good, someone will publish it. One author sent her manuscript out twenty-eight times, revising and rewriting portions of it five different times during the process. The twenty-ninth publisher accepted it and the book received national acclaim. The word is *persevere!*

If everything in this process works smoothly, your first query letter is answered promptly and your manuscript is accepted by a publisher, you can usually figure on two to two and a half years from the time you started writing your first book to that beautiful day when you stand with the printed book in your hand. With your contract fulfilled, you will receive, as a full-fledged writer, free copies of your book from your publisher. If you wish more, you purchase them at reduced cost. You will find there is a certain satisfaction in paying for your own words.

Is writing worth it? A computerized accounting of your time spent writing and getting a book published might net you as little as five cents an hour for your time and effort, but there is something about walking by a bookstore and seeing *your name* on a book—something about getting a letter from a young reader in some far-off place saying how wonderful your book was—something about knowing that your words and ideas have gone out into the world—yes, there are some things that supersede mere fame and money.

EGO-BOOSTING REWARDS

If—and writing and publishing a book is always a big IF—your book is well received, you may be invited by local bookstores to spend a day autographing your books and boosting your sales. This can be tedious, but it can also be rewarding and does give an author the chance to meet young readers in person.

Another if, if your book proves to be a success with young readers, you will be asked to speak to teachers, librarians, and students. There is no better way to keep up on reading trends and young adult fads, for such engagements always generate new outlooks for a writer. The idea for *Moon and Me* (Hadley Irwin) was a remark overheard in a junior high school hallway.

As you continue with your writing career, you will be asked to conduct workshops for aspiring young writers, for teachers of composition, for reading associations, and for librarians. Too many of such presentations can be a dangerous preoccupation, for you will find yourself doing more talking *about* writing, than *writing*. Be wary of those who talk but don't do!

Nominations for book awards, inclusion on best book lists or on children's choice lists, are, of course, most encouraging to a writer. Most rewarding are the letters you will begin to receive from young readers. When teenagers from across the continent write to tell you how much your book has meant, how enjoyable it was to read, and how they wish you would write more, you know all the effort and disappointments and trying-again were worthwhile. Do try to answer every letter, for after all, writing is sharing your perception and reperception with others.

Rules and Reminders

1. Know your audience.
2. Nothing is wasted.
3. Writing is a process.
4. Show, don't tell.
5. Less is more.
6. When in doubt, cut it out.
7. Lean on the verbs. Easy on adjectives and adverbs. Increase verb density.
8. Don't lull your reader to sleep in the past perfect tense. (had gone)
9. Beware of the "would" syndrome.
10. Use the passive sparingly.
11. Listen to your prose. The eye can be fooled more easily than the ear.
12. Eliminate "falling tears." Let the reader provide the waterworks.
13. Don't become bewitched by "which."
14. Use an exclamation point only if the universe is on fire!
15. Trim the fat.
16. Be consistent with tense changes.
17. Specify generalizations.
18. Don't waste time talking *about* writing or writing about writing. Write!
19. Use friends and family sparingly as critics.
20. Don't trip over dangling modifiers.
21. Give up bridge. Play with words.
22. Listen to critics, but do your own thinking.
23. You're not a writer until you are writing.
24. A professional writer numbers pages.
25. If you can't spell, it won't sell.
26. Avoid dull sentences beginning "There is" and "It is."
27. Each speaker deserves a paragraph.
28. An artist who breaks the rule *knows* the rules.
29. Your characters can make cute remarks. Authors cannot.
30. Listen to people talk. Their speech seldom lasts longer than a

breath.

31. In conversation, use "well's," "er's," "ah's," "you know's" sparingly.
32. Theme is an author's responsibility to the reader.
33. A fancy folder will not sell your book. It's what's inside the folder that counts.
34. Double negatives confuse the reader: "She was not unlike her mother." Instead: "She was like her mother."
35. Be suspicious of any sentence that does not paint a word picture.
36. A rough draft is *what* you want to say. A final draft is *how* you want to say it.
37. Even in the most serious story, tickle your reader's funny bone. Kids like to laugh.
38. Rejection slips hurt for only a moment. The glow of acceptance lasts forever.
39. Look with suspicion on all your favorite sentences. Each sentence must serve the whole.
40. Paper clips do not belong on manuscripts.
41. Some books you can't write because you have not lived long enough.
42. An original idea is nothing more than a new combination of old elements.
43. Action makes character.
44. Keep a scrapbook or large file folder to contain fugitive information.
45. You have five senses. Use them all in your writing.
46. Avoid clichés.
47. Punctuation is governed by rules. Learn the purpose of a punctuation mark.
48. Keep your subject and verb as close together as possible.
49. Prepare for the long haul. The sprinter who jumps the starting gun has to be called back to start over.
50. Write on!

APPENDIX

◆

IN A NUTSHELL,
OR
MOST ASKED QUESTIONS
AND THEIR ANSWERS

Q. I have never written before, but I have a good idea for a book. How do I start?

A. First, learn your craft. You would not expect a premed student to perform an intricate organ transplant or brain operation. No more should you expect to write a novel until you have perfected your skills. Start by keeping a daily journal or by writing a paragraph a day and revising it until it says exactly what you mean to say. Read! Read! Read what other good authors have written, being aware of their techniques. Begin by writing short expository pieces: how-to's, informative, historical. Try submitting short fillers or brief how-to's to smaller magazines or to inspirational markets. Play with words until you are aware of the possibilities that lie in the language, and write something every day.

Q. How long must a YA novel be?

A. Long enough to bring life to the page, short enough to provide a teenager with a "good read." Usually a Young Adult novel ranges from 180 to 250 pages or 40,000 to 60,000 words plus. Basically there is no set length.

Q. Several Creative Writing classes are held in my area. One is offered in the Adult Education programs in the public school and the other at an area college. Are these worthwhile and will they make me a better writer?

A. A great deal depends upon the amount of writing the class prompts you to do and upon the experience of the teacher. Association with other writers and would-be writers is often helpful. Sometimes at the end of the course, students get together to read and criticize each other's manuscripts. You will learn discipline in a creative writing class: handing in a piece of writing at a certain deadline. Eventually this imposed discipline can develop into your own self-discipline.

183

Q. I have a friend who is a published writer. May I ask her to read my manuscript and give suggestions?

A. Professional writers prefer to write rather than spend valuable time critiquing someone else's work. It is often an imposition to ask a writer to do this, but if your friend agrees, certainly offer a reading fee. A dollar a page is a fair average of what professionals get for this kind of read-through and critique.

Q. Should I have my book copyrighted before I submit it to a publisher so that no one will steal my idea?

A. There is no need to copyright material since, according to the new copyright law, material is under copyright the moment it is created. The likelihood of someone stealing your idea is negligible. Ideas are like pollen that floats around in the air. What gives you an idea may be giving the same idea to someone else at the same time. Far more important than the idea itself is what you do with it after you have it and how soon you get to work on it. While you are congratulating yourself on having such a keen idea, some other person may have written 10,000 words.

Q. What is the best way to mail my manuscript?

A. First Class is best, but it's also the most expensive. Although the chances of having your manuscript go astray in the mail or be destroyed somewhere along the line is slim, insurance is not a bad idea. If you had your book professionally typed, insurance would cover the cost of having it retyped as well as the cost of the paper and postage. If you did the retyping yourself, an insurance payment would lessen the pain of loss.

Q. How many times should I submit my book to publishers before I give up?

A. There is no definite answer because it would take you several years to exhaust the possibilities of markets. Presumably, long before you reach the end of your list you will have had some indication of the book's merit or lack of it. While a long string of rejections should not make you give up all hope, such responses as "Sorry. Try us again" or "All of us here liked your book, but we're not buying any YA books for our list at this time" would make most authors' hearts leap with joy.

Q. If no publisher is interested in my novel, should I pay to have it published? My fourteen-year-old niece read it and likes it a lot. So does my husband and my mother-in-law, both of whom are great readers.

A. Publishing houses that take money to print your book, instead of houses that pay YOU for the privilege, are lumped under the generic title *Vanity Press*. Unless you have money to spare, an overwhelming desire to see your name on the spine of a book, or plenty of storage space in your attic, forget it. Members of one's own family are most unreliable judges of a book's merit.

Q. Should a beginning writer try to find a literary agent?

A. As a rule, reputable literary agents do not take clients who have not already sold a book or who have not demonstrated some prospect of doing so. However, this should not discourage a beginning writer from trying. Check in the reference section of your library for *Literary Market Place* or *Fiction Writer's Market* or *Literary Agents: How to Get and Work with the Right One for You* (Michael Larsen) for recommendations in locating an agent. A literary agent has personal access to publishers and their immediate needs. Submission through an agent provides a more professional approach to marketing. You as a writer are spared the hassle of sending out query letters, sample chapters, or complete manuscript. Agents also take care of obtaining a contract and selling other rights such as paperback, TV, movie rights, and foreign printings. The fee is usually 10 percent of the royalty payment, including the advance.

Q. Are expenses in writing deductible for income tax purposes?

A. Yes, if you keep an accurate account of postage, paper, major purchases, etc. Deducting office space in your home is a bit more complex. Consult a tax expert.

Q. What is the best advice you can give a beginning author?

A. Read! Read! Read! Write! Write! Write!

SUGGESTED READING

◆

MAGAZINES/BULLETINS

The ALAN Review. Assembly on Literature for Adolescents, National Council of Teachers of English, 1111 Kenyon Rd., Urbana, IL 61801.

Booklist. The American Library Association, 50 E. Huron St., Chicago, IL 60601.

Bulletin of the Center for Children's Books. Ed. Zena Sutherland. University of Chicago Press, 5801 Ellis Ave., Chicago, IL 60637.

The Horn Book Magazine. The Horn Book, Inc., Park Square Building, 31 St. James Ave., Boston, MA 92116.

Interracial Books for Children Bulletin. Council on Interracial Books for Children, 1841 Broadway, New York, NY 10023.

Kirkus Reviews. Kirkus Service, Inc., 200 Park Ave. South, New York, NY 10003.

Media and Methods. North American Publishing Co., 401 N. American Building, 491 N. Broad St., Philadelphia, PA 19108.

The New York Times Book Review. New York Times Co., Times Square, New York, NY 10036.

School Library Journal. R.R. Bowker Co., 1180 Avenue of the Americas, New York, NY 10036.

Voice of Youth Advocates (VOYA), 10 Landing Lane, Room 6M, New Brunswick, NY 08901.

Wilson Library Bulletin. H.W. Wilson Co., 1950 University Ave., Bronx, NY 19452.

Writer's Digest. F&W Publications, Inc., 1507 Dana Ave., Cincinnati, OH 45207.

The Writer. The Writer, Inc., 8 Arlington St., Boston, MA 02116.

WRITING YOUNG ADULT NOVELS

BOOKS

Awards and Prizes. Children's Book Council, New York (published annually).

Bartlett's Familiar Quotations, 15th ed. Ed. Emily Beck. Boston: Little, Brown Co., 1980.

Bettelheim, Bruno. *The Uses of Enchantment: The Meaning and Importance of Fairy Tales.* New York: Knopf, 1976.

Carlsen, G. Robert. *Books and the Teen-Age Reader,* 2nd rev. New York: Harper & Row, 1980, Bantam, 1980.

Cline, Ruth K., and W.G. McBride. *A Guide to Literature for Young Adults.* Glenview, Illinois: Scott, Foresman & Co., 1983.

Columbia-Viking Desk Encyclopedia, 3rd ed. Ed. William Bridgewater. New York: Viking Press, 1968.

Donelson, K.L., and A.P. Nilsen. *Literature for Today's Young Adults.* Glenview, Illinois: Scott, Foresman & Co., 1980.

Evans, Bergen. *Dictionary of Quotations.* New York: Harcourt, Brace, 1954.

Forster, E.M. *Aspects of the Novel.* New York: Harcourt, Brace, 1954.

Gardner, John. *On Becoming a Novelist.* New York: Harper & Row, 1985.

Henry, Laurie, *et al. Fiction Writer's Market,* Cincinnati: Writer's Digest Books, 1988.

Hogrefe, Pearl. *The Process of Creative Writing,* 3rd ed. New York: Harper & Row, 1963.

Horowitz, Lois. *A Writer's Guide to Research.* Cincinnati: Writer's Digest Books, 1985.

Macauley & Larning. *Technique in Fiction.* New York: Harper & Row, 1964.

Neff, Glenda Tennant, *et al. Writer's Market.* Cincinnati: Writer's Digest Books, 1988.

Polking, Kirk. *A Beginner's Guide to Getting Published.* Cincinnati: Writer's Digest Books, 1986.

Reed, Althea. *Reaching Adolescents: The Young Adult Book and the School.* New York: Holt, Rinehart & Winston, 1985.

Rudman, Masha K. *Children's Literature: An Issues Approach.* New York: Longman, Inc., 1976, 1984.

Strunk, William, Jr., and E.B. White. *Elements of Style,* 3rd ed. New York: Macmillan Co., 1979.

Sutherland, Zena, *et al. Children and Books,* 6th ed. Glenview, Illinois: Scott, Foresman & Co., 1981.

Whitlock, Baird W. *From These Beginnings: Openings of 50 Major Literary Works.* New York: Schocken Books, 1985.

Writer's Yearbook. Cincinnati: Writer's Digest Books, 1988.

World Almanac and Book of Facts. New York: World Almanac Pub., 1988.

World Atlas. Chicago: Rand McNally, 1968.

Wyndham/Madison. *Writing for Children and Teenagers.* Cincinnati: Writer's Digest Books, 1986.

Yolen, Jane. *Writing Books for Children,* rev. Boston: The Writer Inc., 1983.

INDEX

A

Accuracy of story background
  in descriptions of dress, language, and history, 81
  and necessary adjustments, 81
  true periods and settings for, 81
Adolescent literature writers. *See* Writing for young adults
Adolescent novels
  appealing to both sexes in, 28
  in the fifties, 4
  first true, 3-4
  as models for coping with life, 85
  in the sixties, 4
  as sources of sex education, 85
Adult characters
  book length influencing development of, 70
  real (developed) and "stock," 70
  roles of, in lives of the young, 70
Adventure story
  action-packed and fast-paced, 16
  examples of, 16
  rules for writing of, 16
Age differences
  author memories main answer to, 29
  bridging the gap of, 29
  between writer and reader, 29
  See also Biases, unconscious
Agents, literary, 185
Alcott, Louisa May, 3
Alger, Horatio, 165
Anachronisms
  avoidance of requiring research, 83
  and wrong time placement, 83
Aristotle
  on art, 165
  on plot construction, 133
Asian youth as readers, 24
Attributives
  dealing with, 93-95
  definition of, 93
Awards for YA writers, 6-7

B

Beginning of book
  components of, 62, 133
  creating a setting in, 55
  establishing a point of view in, 50
  establishing in, the who? what? where? when? 55
  importance of first page in, 54, 115
  indicating the time in, 55
  naming the characters in, 54
  summary of requirements for, 64-65
  See also Opening passages; Point of view
Biases, unconscious
  as agism, 169
  of authors may infiltrate writing, 166
  and change from simplistic YA books, 165-71
  as racism, 168-69
  as sexism in role assignment, 166-68
Black youth as readers, 24
Body of book, 103, 116, 133
Book, the finished product
  and getting it published, 173
  and the neophyte writer's problems, 173
  selecting a market for, 173-74
Book ideas
  potential of in hobbies and interests, 35
  random notions as the start of, 33-34
  seen as previously undiscovered islands, 34
  sources of, 34-36
Business letter form, 175-76

C

Censorship in YA literature, 83-87, 99-100

Chapter divisions
  as "chunks," 121
  creating movement and tension by, 119
  examples of, 119-20
  last lines of, 120
  variations in treatment of, 120
Character, building
  to create "real" people, 74
  examples of, 75-77
  for possible sequels, 74
  by showing growth, 78-79
  by showing motivation, 78
  summary of methods of, 79
Characterization
  age as factor in, 68
  in analogy of book to stock company, 67
  avoiding extremes in, 69
  need for physical descriptions in, 68
  reader recognition accomplished by, 69
  serious character defects avoided in, 69
  stereotypes in, 67
  See also Adult characters; Name selection
Chinese youth as readers, 24
Chunks, 121
Clichés
  as lazy language, 114
  use of outside help in identifying, 114
Coauthoring, 1-2
Coincidence
  more than one seen as weakening book, 105
Complications and subplots
  definition of, 107
  examples of, 106-08
  getting attention through tension, 106
Conflict as element in writing, 104-06
Conservatism in YA book content, 85-86
Cultural differences of young readers, 24

Cursing in YA books
  as handicap to sales, 87
  strictest censorship of, not realistic, 87
  See also Language, foul

D

Decisions
  defined, 50
  and importance of writer's point of view, 50
"Deep thinking"
  adding substance and authenticity to writing, 30
  dredging up childhood memories, 30-32
  how to practice, 30
Denouement, 107, 134
Dialect in YA literature
  flavor of through speech rhythms, 99
  how to write, 99
  regional and ethnic, 99
Dialogue, printed
  differences of, from usual speech, 91, 95, 96
  mechanics of, 91, 98-101
  punctuation of, 95-97
  purposes of, 91, 98-101
  rules and examples of, 95-97
  use of, to create characters, 92, 98
Disclaimers
  and care in selection of name, 72
  when needed, 72
Dress, fads, and slang
  awareness of, 82
  examples of, 82, 93

E

Editors' revisions
  based on market acceptance, 162
  value of, to writer, 162-63

Enclosures with query letter, 176-77
Ending for book
  epilogue as, 138
  and "graphing" the book, 133-34
  happy ever after, 136
  negative, 137
  positive and hopeful, 136
  reader involvement in, 139
  reversal or surprise in, 139
  sad and downbeat, 136
  satisfactory, 136
  symbolism in, 140
  wrap-up of theme in, 140
Ethnic cross-cultural books
  examples of, 18
  importance of accuracy and realism in, 17
  language often a problem in, 18
  as needed addition to YA literature, 17
  by writers drawing on own heritage, 17

F

Fads, 82-83
Family problems treated in YA literature, 25-26
Fear in fiction
  Alfred Hitchcock and, 31
  Judy Blume and, 31
  using writer's memories of, 31-32
Fees for professional readers, 99
Fiction Writer's Market, 177, 185
Flashback. *See* Transition
Flea hop. *See* Transition
Forster, E.M., *Aspects of the Novel*, 105
Frankau, Pamela, *Pen to Paper, a Novelist's Notebook*, 115, 118

G

Galley proofs
  as last chance for corrections, 163
  and need to keep changes minimal, 163

Gender gap in YA literature
  boys as nonreaders of girls' books, 27
  girls as readers of boys' books, 27
  gradual disappearance of, 27
Genre choices
  adventure stories, 16
  ethnic cross-cultural books, 17-18
  historical romances, 18-19
  mysteries, 13-14
  myths and fantasies, 14-15
  peer influence on choice of, 12
  problem/character novels, 12-13
  science fiction, 14-15
  selection of and criteria for, 11-12

H

Hardy Boys series still read, 3
Hemingway, Ernest, 130
Hispanic youth as readers, 24
Historical romance
  basic tenets of, 19
  definition of, 18
  examples of, 19
  importance of research in, 19, 47
  making history come alive in, 18
  popularity of, with both adults and young readers, 18
Hitchcock, Alfred, 31
Homosexuality
  as sensitive subject, 86
  and slow emergence in YA books, 85-86

I

Ibsen, Henrik, 137
Ideas. *See* Book ideas
Indian youth as readers, 24
Ingenue as book character, 67
Innovation, courage in, 86
Interest
  and ability of reader to relate, 115
  discussion of and examples, 114-15

and hazard of wordiness, 115
holding of, by avoiding over-description, 115
and how to keep readers reading, 114, 115
and importance of pace, 115
Interviews, 43-44
Irony, 91
Italics used to express thoughts, 97

J

Japanese youth as readers, 24
Juvenile literature phenomenon
leading to new library departments for youth, 4
requiring new publishers' catalogs, 4
teachers' attitudes toward, 4
See also Young adult fiction

K

"Kiddie" books
examples and discussion of, 84, 85
YA readers too sophisticated for, 84
Korean youth as readers, 24

L

Language, foul
examples of, and how to handle, 87, 88
no necessity for, in most novels, 86
possible parental reactions to, 87
as shocking to some readers, 86
Laotian youth as readers, 24
Latchkey children, 24
Lengths of books, YA vs. adult, 8
Letters. *See* business letter form; Query letter

Libraries, juvenile, 4
Literary Agents: How to Get and Work with the Right One for You (Michael Larsen), 185
Literary Market Place, 185
Little Women, 3
Long jump as transition, 125
Loose ends of plot
discussion and examples of, 137-38
handling with scenes, not summaries, 137
snipping of, 137
wrapped up by protagonists, 137

M

Manuscript
multiple submissions of, 179
preparation for submission of, 177-79
Marketing the book
patience and persistence required for, 179
query letter's place in, 174-75
secondary rewards of success in, 183
surveying possibilities for, 21, 22
use of *Writer's Market* in, 173, 176, 177
Milne, A.A., 120
Moby Dick, 113
Mood in the YA novel
definition of, 150
tools for creation of, 150-51
Motivation
examples of, 78-79
and fitting characters with conflict, 78
necessity of, for speech or action, 78
Movement through time as story element, 108
Mysteries, YA level
anatomy of, 14
examples of, 14
"fun to read, difficult to write," 13
rules of game in, 13-14

N

Name selection
  examples of, 70
  exercise for, 73
  importance of, 70
  and need for disclaimers, 72
  and need to fit character, 70-71
  sources of, 70-71
Nancy Drew series, 3
Narrator of book
  duty of, as writer, 50-51
  role of, in story, 50-51
Narrator as "I" teller
  effective use of, 54
  first-person point of view of, 53
  the problem of "I," 53-54
Narrator as limited teller
  examples of, 52
  third-person viewpoint of, 52
Newbery, John, medal
  how writer selected for, 6-7
  as "Oscar" for YA writers, 6-7

O

Opening passages of book
  good examples of, 58-64
  low-key examples of, 60-64
Outline of story
  subject to change, 57
  as tool in writing, 57

P

Pacing the YA novel
  description of, 115, 118-19
  importance of, 115
  visual aspects of, 121
Patience in marketing
  with resubmission of work, 179
  with time lag between conception
    and publication, 179

Plagiarism
  defined, 46
  how to avoid, 46
Plot of story
  cause and effect vs. coincidence in,
    105
  made of conflict and obstacles, 104,
    115
  seen as organic, growing with the
    book, 104
Point of story
  analogy to sculptor's armature, 57
  disguised message in, 56
  examples of, 56
  exercises for developing, 56-57
  getting to it, 55
Point of view
  definition of, for writing, 50
  of first-person (I), 53
  of first-person narrator, 53
  importance of choice in, 50
  "leap-frogging" of, 51
  of limited third person (she or he),
    51
  omniscient, 50
Polishing a written work. *See* Revising
    and rewriting
Prejudices. *See* Biases, unconscious
Problem/character novel
  emphasis in, on growth, 13
  examples of, 13
  and its need for contemporary set-
    ting, 13
Proofreading
  general—what to look for, 162
  for grammatical correctness only,
    162
Pruning
  list of suggestions for, 160-61
  by tightening the language, 160
Punctuation of dialogue, 90-97

Q

Query letter
  in business letter form, 175-76
  how to write, 174-75
  as true test of writing ability, 174

Questions
list of, with answers, 183-85
most asked by new writers, 183
Quotations within quotations
examples of, 97
use and rules of, 97

R

Racism. *See* Biases, unconscious
Readers of YA literature
character development in books
for, 69
defects of, 69-70
descriptions of, 29
girls and boys as, 27
growth stages of, 7-8
influences on book choices of, 11-
12
and the "me" factor, 69
photos of young people as reminders to writer, 29
priorities of, 27
recognition of characters by, 69
wants and needs of, 32
and who they are, 23, 28-29
Real world, the
and author's duty to present it as
such, 89
entering YA fiction in the sixties, 4-
5
gradually appearing in ethnic novels, 5
social problems of, depicted, 89
Regionalisms
deletion of, 82
examples of, 81-82
necessity for explanation of, 81-82
Reperception, 37-38
Repertory, 68
Research
for authenticity, 42, 43
through eyes of character, 42
as foundation of all writing, 42
library, 44-45
organizing, 45
sources of, 42-43

using in writing the novel, 46-47
Writer's Guide to Research, (Lois
Horowitz), 43
Revising and rewriting
by editors, 162
in-progress type of, 154, 156
and post-completion break, 153
processes for accomplishing, 2,
153-60
requiring moral strength, 153
Rewards for writers, secondary, 180
Risk in writing for young adults, 85-
86
Romances. *See* Teenage romances
Rules and reminders for YA writers,
180-82

S

Scene
definition of, 108
elements of, 109
samples of, 109-10
Science fiction
continuing popularity of, 15
description of, 15
lure of new frontiers in, 15
recurring themes in, 15
successful writers of, 16
Setting for story
avoidance of purely regional description, 39-40
dress, fads, slang in, 81-83
involving both time and place, 40,
81
risk of overdelineating, 39
shown through characters, 40
styles of speech in, 81
See also Regionalism
Sexism. *See* Biases, unconscious
Sexual content of YA books
attitudes of librarians toward, 85
examples of, 86
in explicit scenes or "offstage," 88
neoconservative rejection of, 85
not taboo, 83-84
as possible source of valid sex education, 84-85

Slang in YA books, 100
Sources, primary
 letters, diaries, journals, 42
 places and people with special information, 43-44
 travel to scene, 43
 writer's experiences, 42
Sources, secondary
 historical societies, 45
 libraries, 44-45
 museums, 45
 newspapers, 44-45
Sports and career stories
 continuing popularity of, 16-17
 examples of, 17
 hero of, as clean-cut and winner, 17
 women as central characters in, 17
Stages of growth in reading, 7-8
Stereotypes, 68, 165-71
Stereotypical story setting
 avoidance of, 40
 examples of, 40
Story structure, 64-65
Structural pacing
 examples of, 116-18
 by indicating perils early, 115
 as need to avoid "clumps" of verbiage, 115
 with scenes, description, and dialogue, 116
 as starting story with a bang, 115
Subconscious, use of. See Deep thinking
Submission of manuscript. See Manuscript
Subplots, 106-07
Sue Barton, Student Nurse, 3-4
Suicide, youth, 36
Summary
 examples of, 111-13
 as nonintrusive necessary information, 112
Symbolism, 140
Synopsis with query letter, 177

T

Taboo writing
 agism as, 168-69
 examples of, 166-69
 racism as, 167-68
 sexism as, 166-67
 See also Sexual content of YA books
Teacher attitudes, 4
Teenage romances
 basic rules in writing, 5, 21
 as booming field, 19, 20
 examples of, 22
 formula for, in series, 20-21
 for girls ten to sixteen, 5, 20
 mixed reviews of, by adults, 20
 as more escape than realistic, 6
 publishers' requirements for, 21
Teenager
 examples of new respect for, 5
 respect reflected in subject matter,
  5
 "typical" teenager nonexistent, 28-
  29
Tense
 past and past perfect, 144
 present, in narrative, 145
 time relations indicated by, 144
Theme
 as evolution of idea, 36
 explanation of, 36-37
 youthful definition of, 36-37
Thoughts, of characters
 expressing, 97
 punctuating, 97
Time
 authenticity in writing about, 40
 as determinant of length, 40
 as part of setting, 40
Title, final
 catchiness of, 41
 examples of, 41
Title, working
 as a beacon or focal point, 41
 book acquires identity through, 41
 drawbacks to, 41
 giving writer sense of direction, 41

Tom Swift series, 3
Tone
    examples of, 147-48
    intentional use of, 147-48
    as subtle revelation of author's attitude, 147
Transition
    back and forth, 131
    the flashback device for, 128-32
    the flea-hop device for, 124-25
    and getting from one time or place to the next, 123, 127
    and how to indicate elapsed time, 123
    the long jump device for, 125
Treasure Island, 3
Trollope, Anthony
    on characterization, 78-79
    on handling a long period of time, 126
    on writing first story, 104
Truth in writing
    and avoiding offensive clichés
    examples of, 170-71
Twain, Mark, 3
Types of YA literature. *See* Genre

V

Vanity press, 184
Vicarious experience from books, 26-27
Vietnamese youth as readers, 24
Vocabulary control, 8
Voice
    choice of, 148-49
    effects of active or passive on reader, 148
    examples of, 148-49

W

Waugh, Evelyn, and transitions, 126
Wharton Edith, on ending book, 135
Winnie the Pooh, 120
Writer's Guide to Research, 43
Writer's Market, 6
Writing awards for YA literature, 7
Writing for young adults
    change in, during the sixties, 4-5
    choosing a genre for, 22
    college courses in, 6
    during the fifties, 4
    importance of honesty, repect, and humor in, 8
    periodicals pointed toward, 6
    preparation for, 47
    quality of craftsmanship required for, 8
    rereading favorites as preparation for, 10
    rules and reminders for, 181-82
    textbooks for, 6
    "what if" as idea starter, 39
    See also Accuracy of story background; Anachronisms; Genre

Y

Young adult fiction. *See* Genre choices; Juvenile literature phenomenon; Writing for young adults
Youth
    adolescent as "in the midst," 23
    at 12-14 years, prototypical readers of YA novels, 23

Other Books of Interest

General Writing Books
    Beginning Writer's Answer Book, edited by Kirk Polking (paper) $12.95
    Getting the Words Right: How to Revise, Edit and Rewrite, by Theodore A. Rees Cheney $14.95
    How to Increase Your Word Power, by the editors of Reader's Digest $19.95
    How to Write a Book Proposal, by Michael Larsen $9.95
    Just Open a Vein, edited by William Brohaugh $15.95
    Pinckert's Practical Grammar, by Robert C. Pinckert $14.95
    The 29 Most Common Writing Mistakes & How to Avoid Them, by Judy Delton $9.95
    The Writer's Digest Guide to Manuscript Formats, by Buchman & Groves $16.95
    Writer's Encyclopedia, edited by Kirk Polking (paper) $16.95
    Writer's Guide to Research, by Lois Horowitz $9.95
    Writer's Market, edited by Glenda Neff $21.95

Nonfiction Writing
    Basic Magazine Writing, by Barbara Kevles $16.95
    How to Sell Every Magazine Article You Write, by Lisa Collier Cool $14.95

Fiction Writing
    Creating Short Fiction, by Damon Knight (paper) $8.95
    Fiction is Folks: How to Create Unforgettable Characters, by Robert Newton Peck (paper) $8.95
    Fiction Writer's Market, edited by Laurie Henry $18.95
    How to Write & Sell Your First Novel, by Oscar Collier with Frances Spatz Leighton $14.95
    Storycrafting, by Paul Darcy Boles (paper) $9.95
    Writing the Modern Mystery, by Barbara Norville $15.95

Special Interest Writing Books
    The Children's Picture Book: How to Write It, How to Sell It, by Ellen E.M. Roberts (paper) $15.95
    Comedy Writing Secrets, by Melvin Helitzer $16.95
    The Craft of Comedy Writing, by Sol Saks $14.95
    How to Sell & Re-Sell Your Writing, by Duane Newcomb $10.95
    How to Write Tales of Horror, Fantasy & Science Fiction, edited by J.N. Williamson $15.95
    How to Write & Sell a Column, by Raskin & Males $10.95
    How to Write & Sell Your Personal Experiences, by Lois Duncan (paper) $9.95
    How to Write the Story of Your Life, by Frank P. Thomas $14.95
    Nonfiction for Children: How to Write It, How to Sell It, by Ellen E.M. Roberts $16.95
    Poet's Market, by Judson Jerome $17.95
    Travel Writer's Handbook, by Louise Zobel (paper) $10.95
    Writing Short Stories for Young People, by George Edward Stanley $15.95

The Writing Business
    A Beginner's Guide to Getting Published, edited by Kirk Polking $10.95
    Complete Guide to Self-Publishing, by Tom & Marilyn Ross $19.95
    How to Bulletproof Your Manuscript, by Bruce Henderson $9.95
    How to Write Irresistible Query Letters, by Lisa Collier Cool $10.95
    How You Can Make $25,000 a Year Writing (No Matter Where You Live), by Nancy Edmonds Hanson $15.95
    Literary Agents: How to Get & Work with the Right One for You, by Michael Larsen $9.95
    Professional Etiquette for Writers, by William Brohaugh $9.95

To order directly from the publisher, include $2.00 postage and handling for 1 book and 50¢ for each additional book. Allow 30 days for delivery.

Writer's Digest Books, Dept. B, 1507 Dana Avenue, Cincinnati, Ohio 45207
Credit card orders call TOLL-FREE 1-800-543-4644 (Outside Ohio)
1-800-551-0884 (Ohio only) Prices subject to change without notice.

For information on how to receive Writer's Digest Books at special Book Club member prices, please write to:
Promotion Manager, Writer's Digest Book Club, 1507 Dana Avenue, Cincinnati, Ohio 45207